THE FBI

A Centennial History, 1908-2008

U.S. Department of Justice
Federal Bureau of Investigation

For sale by the Superintendent of Documents, U.S. Government Printing Office
Internet: bookstore.gpo.gov Phone: toll free (866) 512-1800; DC area (202) 512-1800
Fax: (202) 512-2104 Mail: Stop IDCC, Washington, DC 20402-0001

ISBN 978-0-16-080954-5

Acknowledgments

This book was prepared by the
Online/Print Media Unit
Office of Public Affairs
Federal Bureau of Investigation

Robert S. Mueller, III, Director, FBI
John J. Miller, Assistant Director, Office of Public Affairs, FBI
Michael P. Kortan, Deputy Assistant Director, Office of Public Affairs, FBI

Special thanks to:

Michael J. Lilly, Unit Chief, Online/Print Media Unit
John F. Fox, Jr., FBI Historian
Scott T. Carmine, Visual Information Specialist
Tamara R. Harrison, Writer/Editor
Maureen F. Grenke, Writer/Editor
Jonathan T. Cox, Management and Program Analyst
Susan M. Dreweke, Elisa M. Stewart, Writers/Researchers

Photo Credits:

Page 1, Library of Congress, Prints & Photographs Division; Page 2, upper left, Library of Congress, Prints & Photographs Division; Page 4, lower right, Library of Congress, Prints & Photographs Division; Page 9, lower middle, Library of Congress, Prints & Photographs Division; Page 10, lower left, Library of Congress, Prints & Photographs Division; Page 13, top, Library of Congress, World-Telegram photo; Page 13, bottom, Library of Congress, Prints & Photographs Division; Page 30; lower left, AP Photo; Page 32; National Archives; Page 33, National Archives; Page 46, AP Photo; Page 50, National Archives; Page 53, top, AP Photo; Page 54, AP Photo; Page 56; lower left, AP Photo; Page 60, lower left, AP Photo; Page 62, lower right, Library of Congress, World-Telegram photo; Page 64, AP Photo; Page 69, Robert Maass/CORBIS; Page 75, Bettmann/CORBIS; Page 76, AP Photo; Page 80, AP Photo; Page 81, AP Photo; Page 82, REUTERS; Pages 84-85, AP Photo; Page 86, REUTERS, Page 87, REUTERS; Page 88, above right, REUTERS; Page 89, top and right, Twentieth Century Fox Film Corp.; Page 91, AP Photo; Page 92, Bettmann/CORBIS; Page 93, AP Photo; Page 96, left, AP Photo; Page 98, REUTERS; Page 99, left, AP Photo; Page 99, right, REUTERS; Page 100, AP Photo; Pages 102-103, Bettmann/CORBIS; Page 104, *The Washington Post*; Page 105, REUTERS; Page 106, AP Photo; Page 107, AP Photo; Page 111, REUTERS; Page 113, AP Photo.

Inside back cover: *The Gainesville Sun*, Tracy Wilcox. Photograph shows members of the FBI Jacksonville Evidence Response Team, including an officer from the Alachua County Sheriff's Department. The team is transporting surveying equipment to a helicopter that was flown to the scene of double homicide in the Ocala National Forest outside of Ocala, Florida, in January 2006.

All other photographs and images are from the FBI collection.

Dedication

Dedicated to the men and women of the FBI,

who over the past century have made countless sacrifices

and put themselves in harm's way every day

to protect the people and defend the nation.

Contents

Foreword

On July 26, 2008, the FBI celebrates its 100th anniversary as a crime fighting and national security agency dedicated to protecting America and the international community from a world of dangers.

As you will see, since its earliest days there really hasn't been the investigative equivalent of a dull moment for the FBI. Each point in Bureau history has had its own cast of colorful characters, its own investigative challenges and controversies, its own milestones and major cases.

Here on these pages, for example, you will read about that warm summer night when, with FBI agents closing in outside the Biograph Theater in Chicago, the hard-bitten bank robber John Dillinger drew his gun for the last time. You will come across secret-stealing spies, with their hidden messages in hollowed-out nickels and childrens' dolls. You will encounter historic figures like Charles Bonaparte, the progressive attorney general who got it all started, and J. Edgar Hoover, the long-lasting director who turned the FBI into a household name. You will find Watergate and Waco, Murder Inc. and Mississippi Burning, Al Capone and al Qaeda.

But if you look over the full sweep of FBI history, you will see an organization that has come a long way—starting as a tentative experiment, maturing and evolving at every step, learning from successes and stumbles alike,

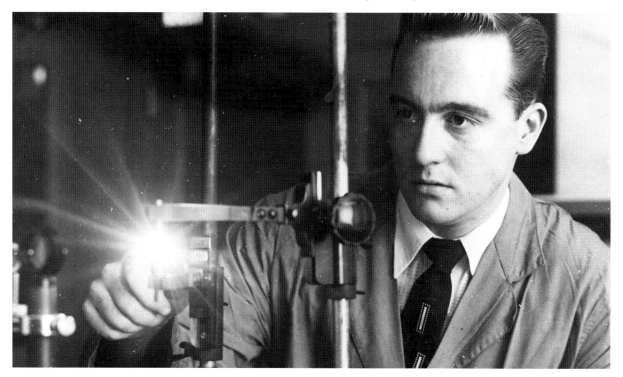

Sleuths of Science: Since the 1930s, the FBI has helped pioneer the application of scientific principles and techniques to solving cases and catching spies, terrorists, and criminals of all kinds.

gaining experience from the latest threat du jour—from gangsters to mobsters, from spies to serial killers, from Internet predators to international terrorists.

Over the century, the FBI has constantly added to its investigative and intelligence tools and talents—launching a Disaster Squad one decade, a "Most Wanted" list the next; a computer forensics team one decade, a terrorist fly team the next—each innovation building on the last like so many foundation stones.

Over time it has become expert at mapping crime scenes and surveiling targets; at poring over financial ledgers and diving into the depths in search of clues; at staging complex undercover operations and breaking cryptic codes; at peering into human cells to help determine guilt or innocence and using intelligence to get its arms around a threat and then disable it. As a result, the FBI has developed a suite of capabilities that is unmatched in any other single national security agency in the world.

At the same time, one common thread for the FBI through the years has been its penchant for lifting all boats in the global law enforcement and intelligence communities. Its rising tide has been a slew of institutionalized training programs and specialized courses. It has been the FBI Laboratory and its quest to apply the discipline and tools of science to the work of solving crimes—and to share its knowledge and services worldwide. It has been its growing collection of national criminal justice services, everything from criminal records to crime reports, from fingerprints to firearms checks.

And more recently, it has been the Bureau's melding into countless joint operations and task forces with an alphabet

soup of agencies—nationally and internationally—where it adds its skills and resources to the collective mix, working together to stop terrorism, cyber crime, and other global dangers, to the point that it is nearly impossible to

separate the contributions of one agency—and even one nation—from the next.

Looking back over this first chapter in the FBI's history, we can see that the experiment of a national investigative force has worked—and worked well enough that the FBI, though far from perfect, is considered a leader and a premier agency of its kind.

For the men and women of the FBI, whose personal sacrifices have been immeasurable, it has been a century to remember…and one to learn from as it walks forward into the future, where new challenges surely await.

Since the late 1920s, FBI agents have undergone rigorous training in firearms, investigative techniques, ethics, and other areas. Today, new agent training lasts 20 weeks.

The Nation Calls, *1908-1923*

B y 1908, the time was right for a new kind of agency to protect America.

The United States was, well, *united*, with its borders stretching from coast to coast and only two landlocked states left to officially join the union. Inventions like the telephone, the telegraph, and the railroad had seemed to shrink its vast distances even as the country had spread west. After years of industrializing, America was wealthier than ever, too, and a new world power on the block, thanks to its naval victory over Spain.

But there were dark clouds on the horizon.

The country's cities had grown enormously by 1908—there were more than 100 with populations over 50,000—and understandably, crime had grown right along with them. In these big cities, with their many overcrowded tenements filled with the poor and disillusioned and with all the ethnic tensions of an increasingly immigrant nation stirred in for good measure, tempers often flared. Clashes between striking workers and their factory bosses were turning increasingly violent.

And though no one knew it at the time, America's cities and towns were also fast becoming breeding grounds for a future generation of professional lawbreakers. In Brooklyn, a nine-year-old Al Capone would soon start his life of crime. In Indianapolis, a five-year-old John Dillinger was growing up on his family farm. And in Chicago, a young child christened Lester Joseph Gillis—later to morph into the vicious killer "Baby Face" Nelson—would greet the world by year's end.

But violence was just the tip of the criminal iceberg. Corruption was rampant nationwide—especially in local politics, with crooked political machines like Tammany Hall in full flower.

Big business had its share of sleaze, too, from the shoddy, even criminal, conditions in meat packaging plants and factories (as muckrakers like Upton Sinclair had so artfully exposed) to the illegal monopolies threatening to control entire industries.

Criminals, start your engines: In 1908, the first Model Ts began rolling off the assembly lines, giving crooks both a tool and a target for crime.

June 29, 1908
Attorney General Bonaparte begins hiring special agent force

President Roosevelt's Cabinet. Attorney General Bonaparte is the third from the left.

The technological revolution was contributing to crime as well. 1908 was the year that Henry Ford's Model T first began rolling off assembly lines in Motor City, making automobiles affordable to the masses and attractive commmodities for thugs and hoodlums, who would soon begin buying or stealing them to elude authorities and move about the country on violent crime sprees. Twenty-two years later, on a dusty Texas back road, Bonnie and Clyde—"Romeo and Juliet in a Getaway Car," as one journalist put it—would meet their end in a bullet-ridden Ford.

Just around the corner, too, was the world's first major global war—compelling America to protect its homeland from both domestic subversion and international espionage and sabotage. America's approach to national security, once the province of cannons and warships, would never be the same again.

President Teddy Roosevelt

Despite it all, in the year 1908 there was hardly any systematic way of enforcing the law across this now broad landscape of America. Local communities and even some states had their own police forces, but at that time they were typically poorly trained, politically appointed, and underpaid. And nationally, there were few federal criminal laws and likewise only a few thinly staffed federal agencies like the Secret Service in place to tackle national crime and security issues.

One of these issues was anarchism—an often violent offshoot of Marxism, with its revolutionary call to overthrow capitalism and bring power to the common man. Anarchists took it a step further—they wanted to do away with government entirely. The prevailing anarchistic creed that government was oppressive and repressive, that it should be overthrown by random attacks on the ruling class (including everyone from police to priests to politicians), was preached by often articulate spokesmen and women around the world. There were plenty who latched onto the message, and by the end of the nineteenth century, several world leaders were among those who had been assassinated.

The anarchists, in a sense, were the first modern-day terrorists—banding together in small, isolated groups around the world; motivated by ideology; bent on bringing down the governments they hated. But they would, ironically, hasten into being the first force of federal agents that would later become the FBI.

It happened at the hands of a 28-year-old Ohioan named Leon Czolgosz, who after losing his factory job and turning to the writings of anarchists like Emma Goldman and Alexander Berkman, took a train to Buffalo, bought a revolver, and put a bullet in the stomach of a visiting President McKinley.

Eight days later, on September 14, 1901, McKinley was dead, and his vice president Teddy Roosevelt took the oval office.

Call it Czolgosz's folly, because this new President was a staunch advocate of the rising "Progressive Movement." Many progressives, including Roosevelt, believed that the federal government's guiding hand was necessary to foster justice in an industrial society. Roosevelt, who had no tolerance for corruption and little trust of those he called the "malefactors of great wealth," had already cracked the whip of reform for six years as a Civil Service Commissioner in Washington (where, as he said, "we stirred things up well") and for two years as head of the New York Police Department. He was a believer in the law and in the enforcement of that law, and it was under his reform-driven leadership that the FBI would get its start.

Attorney General Charles J. Bonaparte

July 26, 1908
Force reports to Chief Examiner, formal beginning of future FBI

Office of the Attorney General,
Washington, D.C

July 26, 1908.

ORDER

All matters relating to investigations under the Department, except those to be made by bank examiners, and in connection with the naturalization service, will be referred to the Chief Examiner for a memorandum as to whether any member of the force of special agents under his direction is available for the work to be performed. No authorization of expenditure for special examinations shall be made by any officer of the Department, without first ascertaining whether one of the regular force is available for the service desired, and, in case the service cannot be performed by the regular force of special agents of the Department, the matter will be specially called to the attention of the Attorney General, or Acting Attorney General, together with a statement from the Chief Examiner as to the reasons why a regular employee cannot be assigned to the work, before authorization shall be made for the expenditure of any money for this purpose.

CHARLES J. BONAPARTE,

Attorney General.

It all started with a short memo, dated July 26, 1908, and signed by Charles J. Bonaparte, Attorney General, describing a "regular force of special agents" available to investigate certain cases of the Department of Justice. This memo is celebrated as the official birth of the Federal Bureau of Investigation—known throughout the world today as the FBI.

March 1909
Named Bureau of Investigation

June 25, 1910
White Slave Traffic Act passed

The Bureau's first home, the Department of Justice building at 1435 K Street in N.W. Washington, D.C.

given the jobs to the survivors." Roosevelt soon grew to trust this short, stocky, balding man from Baltimore and appointed Bonaparte to a series of posts during his presidency.

Soon after becoming the nation's top lawman, Bonaparte learned that his hands were largely tied in tackling the rising tide of crime and corruption. He had no squad of investigators to call his own except for one or two special agents and other investigators who carried out specific assignments on his behalf. They included a force of examiners trained as accountants who reviewed the financial transactions of the federal courts and some civil rights investigators. By 1907, when he wanted to send an investigator out to gather the facts or to help a U.S. Attorney build a case, he was usually borrowing operatives from the Secret Service. These men were well trained, dedicated—and expensive. And they reported not to the Attorney General, but to the Chief of the Secret Service. This situation frustrated Bonaparte, who had little control over his own investigations.

Stanley W. Finch

Bonaparte made the problem known to Congress, which wondered why he was even renting Secret Service investigators at all when there was no specific provision in the law for it. In a complicated, political showdown with Congress, involving what lawmakers charged was Roosevelt's grab for executive power, Congress banned the loan of Secret Service operatives to any federal department in May 1908.

Attorney General George W. Wickersham

Now Bonaparte had no choice, ironically, but to create his own force of investigators, and that's exactly what he did in the coming weeks, apparently with Roosevelt's blessing. In late June, the Attorney General quietly hired nine of the Secret Service investigators he had borrowed before and brought them together with another 25 of his own to form a special agent force. On July 26, 1908, Bonaparte ordered Department of Justice attorneys to refer most investigative matters to his Chief Examiner, Stanley W. Finch, for handling by one of these 34 agents. The new force had its mission—to conduct investigations for the Department of Justice—so that date is celebrated as the official birth of the FBI.

The chain of events was set in motion in 1906, when Roosevelt appointed a likeminded reformer named Charles Bonaparte as his second Attorney General. The grandnephew of the infamous French emperor, Bonaparte was a noted civic reformer. He met Roosevelt in 1892 when they both spoke at a reform meeting in Baltimore. Roosevelt, then with the Commission, talked with pride about his insistence that Border Patrol applicants pass marksmanship tests, with the most accurate getting the jobs. Following him on the program, Bonaparte countered, tongue in cheek, that target shooting was not the way to get the best men. "Roosevelt should have had the men shoot at each other, and

With Congress raising no objections to this new unnamed force as it returned from its summer vacation, Bonaparte kept a close **(continued on page 8)**

APPLICATION FOR APPOINTMENT TO POSITION OF SPECIAL AGENT
OF THE DEPARTMENT OF JUSTICE.

April 22nd, 1909

The Attorney General,
Washington, D. C.

Sir:

Application is hereby made for appointment to the position of Special Agent of the Department of Justice, and for your use in this connection the following information is submitted:

Name, *Geo W. Ribeiro*   Legal residence, *New York City*

Mail and telegraphic address, *#344 Ninth Ave.*

Age on last birthday, *28*   Weight, *18 lbs* Height, *5 ft 8¼ inches*

Nationality, *American*

Marital condition, *Wife*   Number of children, if any, *one boy.*

Address of wife or nearest adult relative, *# 344 - 9th Ave*

New York City

Whether or not applicant uses intoxicating liquors or narcotics, and to what extent, *never use liquors at all, but smoke accasionaly*

Education (stating nature of education, what languages, including English, applicant is able to read, write, and speak, etc.),

Read, write and speak English and German fluently, and also practiced Veterinary Medicine and Surgery.
Passed examination as Pilot for N.Y. Harbor and its inland water on July 27th 1907, my liscense expires July27th 1912.

[OVER.]

This application is accompanied by a recent photograph of the applicant.

Respectfully,

Geo. W. Ribeiro,

...t service
...rom 1901
... by the
... City,
...anage
...to the
...self,
...Broadway
...been
...entered
...Justice
... employ-
...e is
...oyment
...o.171
...No.
...for
...3rd Ave
...shop of Paint
...and East River New York City

April 6, 1917
U.S. enters the war

June 15, 1917
Espionage Act passed

June 30, 1919
William Flynn named Director

The Russian Cossack Turned Special Agent

Emilio Kosterlitzky was one of the most colorful characters to ever serve as a special agent.

A cultured, Russian-born man of the world, he spent four decades in the Russian and Mexican militaries, rising to the rank of brigadier general in Mexico. To avoid the dangerous tribulations of the ongoing Mexican Revolution, he settled down in Los Angeles in 1914.

In 1917, the same year as the Bolshevik revolution in his native land, he joined the FBI. He was 63.

Kosterlitzky was appointed a "special employee," like today's investigative assistant but with more authority. And with his deep military experience and international flair (including strong connections throughout Mexico and the Southwest U.S. and the ability to speak, read, and write more than eight languages) he excelled at it. His work included not only translations but also undercover work.

On May 1, 1922, Kosterlitzky was appointed a Bureau special agent at a salary of six dollars a day. Because of his unique qualifications he was assigned to work border cases and to conduct liaison with various Mexican informants and officials. By all accounts, he showed exceptional diplomacy and skill.

In 1926, Kosterlitzky was ordered to report to the Bureau's office in Phoenix but could not comply because of a serious heart condition. He resigned on September 4, 1926. Less than two years later this grand old gentleman died and was buried in Los Angeles.

Kosterlitsky's oath of office. The cultured Russian-born agent could speak, read, and write more than eight languages.

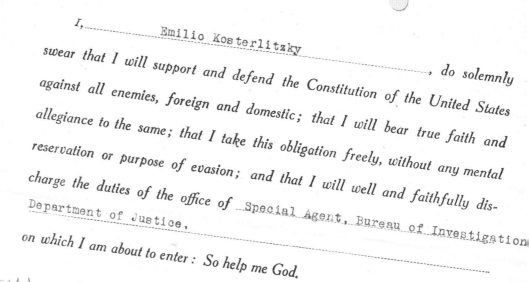

I, _____ Emilio Kosterlitzky _____, do solemnly swear that I will support and defend the Constitution of the United States against all enemies, foreign and domestic; that I will bear true faith and allegiance to the same; that I take this obligation freely, without any mental reservation or purpose of evasion; and that I will well and faithfully discharge the duties of the office of _____ Special Agent, Bureau of Investigation Department of Justice, on which I am about to enter: So help me God.

841

(Sign

The Bureau's First Wanted Poster

On December 2, 1919, a 23-year-old soldier named William N. Bishop slipped out of the stockade at Camp A. A. Humphreys—today's Fort Belvoir—in northern Virginia.

Shortly after Bishop's getaway, the Military Intelligence Division of the Army requested the Bureaus' help in finding him. One early assistant director, Frank Burke, responded by sending a letter to "All Special Agents, Special Employees and Local Officers" asking them to "make every effort" to capture Bishop.

Little did anyone know at the time, but that letter set in motion a chain of events that would forever change how the FBI and its partners fight crime.

In the letter, Burke included every scrap of information that would help law enforcement of the day locate and identify Bishop: a complete physical description, down to the pigmented mole near his right armpit; possible addresses he might visit, including his sister's home in New York; and a "photostat" of a recent portrait taken at "Howard's studio" on seventh street in Washington, D.C.

Burke labeled that document—dated December 15, 1919—"Identification Order No. 1." In essence, it was the Bureau's first wanted poster, and it put the organization squarely in the fugitive-catching business just eleven years into its history. It has been at it ever since.

Within a few years, the identification order—or what soon became known throughout law enforcement as an "IO"—had become a staple of crime fighting. By the late 1920s, these wanted flyers were circulating not only throughout the U.S. but also Canada and Europe (and later worldwide). The IO evolved into a standard 8x8 size, and the Bureau soon added to them fingerprints (thanks to its growing national repository), criminal records, and other background information. By the 1930s, IOs were sent to police stations around the nation, enlisting the eyes of

the public in the search for fugitives. In 1950, building on the "wanted posters" concept, the FBI created its "Ten Most Wanted Fugitives" list.

And what of Mr. Bishop? With the help of the identification order, he was captured less than five months later, on April 6, 1920.

The Bureau's first Identification Order, dated December 15, 1919, put it squarely in the fugitive-catching business.

Female Feds

They were pioneers, the first trio of women known to serve as Bureau special agents and among the first women in federal law enforcement.

All three women did well in training at the New York office and, in general, performed up to standard.

Alaska Davidson and Jessie Duckstein were assigned to the Bureau's Washington field office. Both were dismissed when newly appointed Director J. Edgar Hoover dramatically cut the Bureau rolls in the spring of 1924 to clean house following the Teapot Dome scandals. Lenore Houston was hired after these initial cuts and served the longest of the three. She, too, was assigned to the Washington office. She was asked to resign in 1928.

It would be nearly another half century—May 1972—before social mores would change and women special agents would become a regular and vital part of the FBI.

Who they were:

Alaska P. Davidson,
October 1922
to June 1924

Miss Lenore Houston,
January 1924 to
November 1928

Mrs. Jessie B.
Duckstein,
November 1923
to May 1924
(not pictured)

Houston's credentials

hold on its work for the next seven months before stepping down with his retiring president in early March 1909. A few days later, on March 16, Bonaparte's successor, Attorney General George W. Wickersham, gave this band of agents their first name—the Bureau of Investigation. It stuck.

During its first 15 years, the Bureau was a shadow of its future self. It was not yet strong enough to withstand the sometimes corrupting influence of patronage politics on hiring, promotions, and transfers. New agents received limited training and were sometimes undisciplined and poorly managed. The story is told, for example, of a Philadelphia agent who was for years allowed to split time between doing his job and tending his cranberry bog. Later, a more demanding J. Edgar Hoover reportedly made him chose between the two.

Still, the groundwork for the future was being laid. Some excellent investigators and administrators were hired (like the Russian-born Emilio Kosterlitzky, see page 6), providing a stable corps of talent. And the young Bureau was getting its feet wet in all kinds of investigative areas—not just in law enforcement disciplines, but also in the national security and intelligence arenas.

At first, agents investigated mostly white-collar and civil rights cases, including antitrust, land fraud, banking fraud, naturalization and copyright violations, and peonage (forced labor). It handled a few national security issues as well, including treason and some anarchist activity. This list of responsibilities continued to grow as Congress warmed to this new investigative force as a way to advance its national agenda. In 1910, for example, the Bureau took the investigative lead on the newly passed Mann Act or "White Slave Traffic Act," an early attempt to halt interstate prostitution and human trafficking. By 1915, Congress had increased Bureau personnel more than tenfold, from its original 34 to about 360 special agents and support personnel.

And it wasn't long before international issues took center stage, giving the Bureau its first real taste of national security work. On the border with Mexico, the Bureau had already opened several offices to investigate smuggling and neutrality violations. Then came the war in Europe in 1914. America watched from afar, hoping to avoid entangling alliances and thinking that 4,000 miles worth of ocean was protection enough. But when German subs started openly sinking American ships and German saboteurs began planting bombs on U.S. ships and targeting munitions plants on U.S. soil (see page 10), the nation was provoked into the conflict.

Congress declared war on April 6, 1917, but at that point its own laws were hardly up to the task of protecting the U.S. from subversion and sabotage. So it quickly passed the Espionage Act and later the Sabotage Act and gave responsibility to the principal national investigative agency—the Bureau of Investiga-

October 28, 1919
National Motor Vehicle Theft Act passed

Department of Justice
Bureau of Investigation
Washington, D.C.

November 22 1909

TO WHOM IT MAY CONCERN

This is to certify that the bearer, whose name and photograph appear hereon, is a regularly appointed Special Agent of this Department and as such is charged with the duty of investigating violations of the laws of the United States and collecting evidence in cases in which the United States is, or may be a party in interest.

CHIEF, BUREAU OF INVESTIGATION

ATTORNEY GENERAL

The Earliest Directors

These four men served as the first directors of the Bureau of Investigation before J. Edgar Hoover took the job in May 1924.

**Stanley W. Finch,
1908 to 1912**

**A. Bruce Bielaski,
1912 to 1919**

**William J. Flynn,
1919 to 1921**

**William J. Burns,
1921 to 1924**

tion—putting the agency in the counter-spy business less than a decade into its history. The Bureau also landed the job of rounding up army deserters and policing millions of "enemy aliens"—Germans in the U.S. who were not American citizens—as well as of enforcing a variety of other war-related crimes.

The war would end in November 1918, but it was hardly the end of globally-inspired turmoil within the U.S. The Bolsheviks had taken over Russia in 1917, and Americans soon became nervous about its talk of worldwide revolution, especially in the face of its own widespread labor and economic unrest. A wave of intolerance and even injustice spread across the nation not only against communists but also against other radicals like the "Wobblies," a sometimes violent labor union group called the Industrial Workers of the World. When anarchists launched a series of bombing attacks on national leaders in 1919 and 1920 (see page 12), a full-blown "Red Scare" was on.

Attorney General A. Mitchell Palmer responded with a massive investigation, led by a young Justice Department lawyer named J. Edgar Hoover, who amassed detailed information and intelligence on radicals and their activities. The ensuing "Palmer Raids" were poorly planned and executed and heavily criticized for infringing on the civil liberties of the thousands of people swept up in the raids. The incident provided an important lesson for the young Bureau, and its excesses helped temper the country's attitudes toward radicalism.

A new era of lawlessness, though, was just beginning, and the nation would soon need its new federal investigative agency more than ever. As you'll see in the next chapter, the Bureau first had to get its own house in order.

**Top of page: One of the first special agents credentials
Above: A 1914 protest by the Industrial Workers of the World,
known as the "Wobblies"**

December 15, 1919
Bureau issues first Identification Order

August 22, 1921
William Burns becomes Director; J. Edgar Hoover named Assistant Director

FAMOUS CASES

"Black Tom" Bombing Propels Bureau Into National Security Arena

It was still dark in Manhattan on that Sunday morning, July 30, 1916, when the sky suddenly exploded with an unnatural brilliance. Two million tons of war materials packed into train cars had blown up in the Black Tom railroad yard on what is now a part of Liberty State Park.

Thousands of windows shattered in lower Manhattan and Jersey City. Shrapnel pock-marked the Statue of Liberty. Three men and a baby were killed by the explosive energy that erupted from this act of sabotage.

The culprits? German agents who were determined to prevent American munitions shippers from supplying the English during the First World War. Never mind that the U.S. was officially neutral in the conflict at this point.

How to respond? With difficulty. With few national security laws and no real intelligence community to thwart German agents, America was vulnerable. The Secret Service, by presidential order, was able to investigate some German attacks and intrigues. The Bureau of Investigation likewise did what it could, but it was held back by its small size (260 employees in a handful of offices) and lack of jurisdiction. The most successful and experienced anti-sabotage investigators turned out to be the detectives of the New York Police Department's Bomb Squad—even so, the German agents who blew up Black Tom were not identified at the time.

The Black Tom explosion wasn't the only provocation. When Germany proposed to Mexico that it ally itself with the Kaiser against America…and when it resumed unrestricted submarine warfare on any enemy or neutral ship crossing the Atlantic… America declared war.

Congress immediately passed the Espionage Act of 1917, which outlawed a variety of crimes associated with German agents; passed several other wartime laws; then the following year passed the Sabotage Act. And the Bureau exercised primary jurisdiction over all of these laws as it pursued a wide variety of national security investigations. How successful were they? Very. German intrigues on American soil essentially evaporated.

Postscript: Were the saboteurs ever identified? Oh, yes. The Bureau and other agencies doggedly pursued the case after the war until the saboteurs were identified and, ultimately, reparations were paid for German attacks against our neutral country.

Above: The aftermath of the explosion at Black Tom, which killed three men and a baby and pock-marked the Statue of Liberty
Right: Workers sorting shells at Black Tom

FAMOUS CASES

Patriot Games

The year was 1917, the war was on, and the Bureau was in need of intelligence about the activities of German agents.

After learning that German embassy documents had been secretly stashed in the Swiss Consulate in New York City in order to avoid their capture by U.S. or British intelligence, the Bureau decided to go after them. The head of the Bureau office in New York—Charles De Woody—put five agents on the job.

Charles De Woody

They immediately set to work. The team quickly determined that the documents were locked in a storeroom on the ninth floor of the consulate building. Renting an adjacent office, they waited until embassy employees left one April afternoon and then created a secret tunnel into the locked storeroom. There they found a series of trunks and boxes carefully sealed with red, white, and black tape, ropes, and wax seals. The game was on.

Von Rintelen

After mapping out their operation, the agents snuck into the storeroom every few nights, removed the documents they wanted, and carefully replaced the seals and tape so that no evidence of their tampering remained. By early July, they'd secured thousands of pages of German documents. Closing up operations, they hired a porter who carted the crates of documents to the Justice Department office in New York and left them on the doorstep "anonymously." Translators started transcribing them immediately, and the five recently retired agents returned to work.

The intelligence value of the cache was significant. De Woody reported that the records "disclosed methods by which the enemy was enabled to secure information for delivering war materials and supplies by enemy ships under neutral flags" … and "furnished the United States government with information as to the identity [of] methods of codes and enemy intelligence system activities in this country from the beginning of the war," including the activities of German spy master Von Rintelen and his network.

Above: A German ship transporting war supplies
Below: Account of the operation in the *New York Tribune*

Highly Important Documents, Left by Von Bernstorff in Consulate in New York, Helped Beat Teutons

Five Patriotic Adventurers Seized Them During War

Task Was a Masterpiece of Honest Burglary; Multitude of Seals Removed and Replaced by Ingenious Process

This is the amazing story of how five American adventurers obtained and turned over to the United States government very important secret German papers which the Wilhelmstrasse still believes are in the Swiss Consulate in New York.

Charles F. De Woody, who was chief of the special agents of the Department of Justice for the New York Division, had the custody of the documents and supervised the investigations resulting from them.

Mr. De Woody was shown a copy of this article and said:

"I regard the story as an authentic one."

By Fred C. Kelly

(Copyright, 1920, New York Tribune Inc.)

When diplomatic relations are once more... one of the first acts of Germ... to the Swi...

reached th... ...cials, ... value to th... task of lo... within our ... tivities.

The papers... German Emb... hundreds of le... von Bernstorff... and both the e... from the office... the German fi... von Bernstorff... spondents in th... German-America... and social circle... toward the coun... the public knows

Letters Reveal A... Of German-Ame...

There were stack... Albert and von Ber... mass of letters a... that passed between... ous German agents... ficial ledgers, person... check books and ... showed exactly the a... disbursed to German... of the n...

FAMOUS CASES

The Palmer Raids

The bomb hit home, both literally and figuratively.

On June 2, 1919, a militant anarchist named Carlo Valdinoci blew up the front of newly appointed Attorney General A. Mitchell Palmer's home in Washington, D.C.—and himself up in the process when the bomb exploded too early. A young Franklin and Eleanor Roosevelt, who lived across the street, were also shaken by the blast.

**Attorney General
A. Mitchell Palmer**

The bombing was just one in a series of coordinated attacks that day on judges, politicians, law enforcement officials, and others in eight cities nationwide. About a month earlier, radicals had also mailed bombs to the mayor of Seattle and to a U.S. Senator, blowing the hands off the senator's domestic worker. The next day, a postal worker in New York City intercepted 16 more packages addressed to political and business leaders, including John D. Rockefeller.

It was a time of high anxiety in America—driven by a deadly wave of the pandemic flu, the Bolshevik Revolution in Russia, and sometimes violent labor strikes across the country.

Emma Goldman

The nation demanded a response to the bombings, and the Attorney General—who had his eye on the White House in 1920—was ready to oblige. He created a small division to gather intelligence on the radical threat and placed a young Justice Department lawyer named J. Edgar Hoover in charge. Hoover collected and organized every scrap of intelligence gathered by the Bureau of Investigation and by other agencies to identify anarchists most likely involved in violent activity. The young Bureau, meanwhile, continued to investigate those responsible for the bombings.

Alexander Berkman

Later that fall, the Department of Justice began arresting, under laws that prohibited immigration by foreign anarchists, suspected radicals and foreigners identified by Hoover's group, including well-known leaders Emma Goldman and Alexander Berkman. In December 1919, with much public fanfare, a number of radicals were put on a ship dubbed the "Red Ark" or "Soviet Ark" by the press and deported to Russia.

At this point, though, politics, inexperience, and overreaction got the better of Attorney General Palmer and his department.

Hoover—with the encouragement of Palmer and the help of the Department of Labor—started planning a massive roundup of radicals.

By the start of 1920, the plans were ready. The department organized simultaneous raids in major cities, with local police called on to arrest thousands of suspected anarchists. But the ensuing "Palmer Raids" turned into a nightmare, marked by poor communications, planning, and intelligence about who should be targeted and how many arrest warrants would be needed. The constitutionality of the entire operation was questionable, and Palmer and Hoover were roundly criticized for the plan and for their overzealous domestic security efforts.

The "Palmer Raids" were certainly not a bright spot for the young Bureau. But it did gain valuable experience in terrorism investigations and intelligence work and learn important lessons about the need to protect civil liberties and constitutional rights.

Attorney General A. Mitchell Palmer's home following the blast

FAMOUS CASES

Terror on Wall Street

The lunch rush was just beginning as a non-descript man driving a cart pressed an old horse forward on a mid-September day in 1920. He stopped the animal and its heavy load in front of the U.S. Assay Office, across from the J. P. Morgan building in the heart of Wall Street. The driver got down and quickly disappeared into the crowd.

Within minutes, the cart exploded into a hail of metal fragments—immediately killing more than 30 people and injuring some 300. The carnage was horrific, and the death toll kept rising as the day wore on and more victims succumbed.

Who was responsible? In the beginning it wasn't obvious that the explosion was an intentional act of terrorism. Crews cleaned up the damage overnight, including physical evidence that today would be crucial to identifying the perpetrator. By the next morning Wall Street was back in business—broken windows draped in canvas, workers in bandages, but functioning none-the-less.

Conspiracy theories abounded, but the New York Police and Fire Departments, the Bureau of Investigation, and the U.S. Secret Service were on the job. Each avidly pursued leads. The Bureau interviewed hundreds of people who had been around the area before, during, and after the attack, but developed little information of value. The few recollections of the driver and wagon were vague and virtually useless. The NYPD was able to reconstruct the bomb and its fuse mechanism, but there was much debate about the nature of the explosive, and all the potential components were commonly available.

The most promising lead had actually come prior to the explosion. A letter carrier had found four crudely spelled and printed flyers in the area from a group calling itself the "American Anarchist Fighters" that demanded the release of political prisoners. The letters, discovered later, seemed similar to ones used the previous year in two bombing campaigns fomented by Italian Anarchists (see page 12). The Bureau worked diligently, investigating up and down the East Coast, to trace the printing of these flyers, without success.

Based on bomb attacks over the previous decade, the Bureau initially suspected followers of the Italian Anarchist Luigi Galleani. But the case couldn't be proved, and the anarchist had fled the country. Over the next three years, hot leads turned cold and promising trails turned into dead ends. In the end, the bombers were not identified. The best evidence and analysis since that fateful day of September 16, 1920, suggests that the Bureau's

The scene in New York moments after the blast, which killed more than 30 people and injured some 300

initial thought was correct—that a small group of Italian Anarchists were to blame. But the mystery remains.

FAMOUS CASES

Murder and Mayhem in Osage Hills

In May 1921, the badly decomposed body of Anna Brown—an Osage Native American—was found in a remote ravine in northern Oklahoma. The undertaker later discovered a bullet hole in the back of her head. Anna had no known enemies, and the case went unsolved.

Anna Brown

That might have been the end of it, but just two months later, Anna's mother suspiciously died. Two years later, her cousin Henry Roan was shot to death. Then, in March 1923, Anna's sister and brother-in-law were killed when their home was bombed.

One by one, at least two dozen people in the area inexplicably turned up dead. Not just Osage Indians, but a well-known oilman and others.

What did they all have in common? Who was behind all the murders?

That's what the terrorized community wanted to find out. But a slew of private detectives and other investigators turned up nothing (and some were deliberately trying to sidetrack honest efforts). The Osage Tribal Council turned to the federal government, and Bureau agents were detailed to the case.

Early on, all fingers pointed at William Hale, the so-called "King of the Osage Hills." A local cattleman, Hale had bribed, intimidated, lied, and stolen his way to wealth and power. He grew even greedier in the late 1800s when oil was discovered on the Osage Indian Reservation. Almost overnight, the Osage became incredibly wealthy, earning royalties from oil sales through their federally mandated "head rights."

William Hale

Hale's connection to Anna Brown's family was clear. His weak-willed nephew, Ernest Burkhart, was married to Anna's sister. If Anna, her mother, and two sisters died—in that order—all of the "head rights" would pass to the nephew...and Hale could take control. The prize? Half-a-million dollars a year or more.

Above right: The ravine where Anna Brown's body was discovered. Lower right: Anna's aunt (sitting) and housemaid outside her home.

Solving the case was another matter. The locals weren't talking. Hale had threatened or paid off many of them; the rest had grown distrustful of outsiders. Hale also planted false leads that sent Bureau agents scurrying across the southwest.

So four agents got creative. They went undercover as an insurance salesman, a cattle buyer, an oil prospector, and a herbal doctor to turn up evidence. Over time, they gained the trust of the Osage and built a case. Finally, someone talked. Then others confessed. The agents were able to prove that Hale ordered the murders of Anna and her family to inherit their oil rights, their cousin Roan for the insurance, and others who had threatened to expose him.

In 1929, Hale was convicted and sent to the slammer. His henchmen—including a hired killer and crooked lawyer—also got time. Case closed...and a grateful community safe once more.

Today, more than a hundred FBI agents from 21 field offices investigate cases on some 200 reservations nationwide, working with a range of partners to help tamp down crime and ensure justice on tribal lands.

FAMOUS CASES

Imperial Kleagle of the Ku Klux Klan in Kustody

In mid-March 1924, Edward Young Clarke, an advertising executive in the state of Louisiana, pled guilty in federal court to violating the Mann Act, an anti-prostitution measure enacted in 1910. The fact that he had been caught taking his mistress across state lines, however, was just the tip of this federal case.

Edward Young Clarke

Why was Clarke a wanted man? He was no mere advertising executive. He was an entrepreneur who believed in the tenets of the Ku Klux Klan—which had been resurrected by "Colonel" William S. Simmons in 1915—and he took its anti-Jewish, anti-African-American, and anti-Catholic tenets to heart.

At the same time, he also liked to turn a profit. In 1920 he agreed to aggressively increase membership in the Klan in return for a share of the membership dues. And he was incredibly successful: over one million members signed up in short order.

In 1922, Louisiana Governor John M. Parker had sent J. Edgar Hoover, then Assistant Director of the Bureau of Investigation, a heartfelt message that was personally delivered by a New Orleans newspaper reporter. Please help, it said, the Ku Klux Klan has grown so powerful in my state that it effectively controls the northern half. It has already kidnapped, tortured, and killed two people who opposed it…and it has threatened many more.

Louisiana Governor John M. Parker

How could the Bureau investigate? At the time, of course, federal civil rights laws were few, and the Bureau did not have authority to investigate. KKK cross-burnings and murders were state matters. But Governor Parker petitioned President Harding to act under the constitutional guarantee that the federal government would protect the states from domestic violence (Article 4, Section 4). The President agreed, and the Bureau promptly sent agents to investigate, even though it would likely have to turn its evidence over to state governments to prosecute the cases.

What did the FBI find? It found that the Klan was wielding great political power throughout the South as it fed off the prejudices of the day and instilled fear in millions. It found that Clarke's campaign to increase Klan membership had been a resounding success. Membership had soared and so had the number of Klan groups in many different states.

On a more personal note, it found that "Imperial Kleagle" Clarke had lined his pockets with $8 of each $10 initiation fee he had secured and that he was also netting tidy profits from his new member sales of the Klan's bedsheet regalia, none of

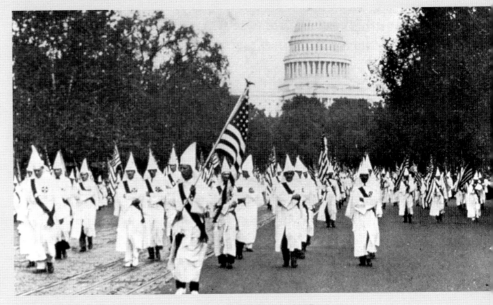

The KKK marching down Pennsylvania Avenue in Washington in 1927

which were violations of federal law. But agents also found that he was using his wealth to lead a high life, including taking on a mistress, and that he was crossing state lines with her.

Now this last was an interesting point. How about using the Mann Act, an enterprising Bureau lawyer suggested. Accordingly, Clarke was arrested when he made his next trip over a state line with his mistress, leading to his guilty plea.

It was just the beginning of the Bureau's fight to bring these early day domestic terrorists to justice.

The FBI and the American Gangster, *1924-1938*

The "war to end all wars" was over, but a new one was just beginning—on the streets of America.

It wasn't much of a fight, really—at least at the start.

On the one side was a rising tide of professional criminals, made richer and bolder by Prohibition, which had turned the nation "dry" in 1920. In one big city alone—Chicago—an estimated 1,300 gangs had spread like a deadly virus by the mid-1920s. There was no easy cure. With wallets bursting from bootlegging profits, gangs outfitted themselves with "Tommy" guns and operated with impunity by paying off politicians and police alike. Rival gangs led by the powerful Al "Scarface" Capone and the hot-headed George "Bugs" Moran turned the city streets into a virtual war zone with their gangland clashes. By 1926, more than 12,000 murders were taking place every year across America.

On the other side was law enforcement, which was outgunned (literally) and ill-prepared at this point in history to take on the surging national crime wave. Dealing with the bootlegging and speakeasies was challenging enough, but the "Roaring Twenties" also saw bank robbery, kidnapping, auto theft, gambling, and drug trafficking become increasingly common crimes. More often than not, local police forces were hobbled by the lack of modern tools and training. And their jurisdictions stopped abruptly at their borders.

In the young Bureau of Investigation, things were not much better. In the early twenties, the agency was no model of efficiency. It had a growing reputation for politicized investigations. In 1923, in the midst of the Teapot Dome scandal that rocked the

Al "Scarface" Capone in a 1929 mug shot

May 10, 1924	July 1, 1924
J. Edgar Hoover appointed acting Director	Bureau begins managing fingerprint files for nation

Harding Administration, the nation learned that Department of Justice officials had sent Bureau agents to spy on members of Congress who had opposed its policies. Not long after the news of these secret activities broke, President Calvin Coolidge fired Harding's Attorney General Harry Daugherty, naming Harlan Fiske Stone as his successor in 1924.

A good housecleaning was in order for the Bureau, and it came at the hands of a young lawyer by the name of J. Edgar Hoover. Hoover had joined the Department of Justice in 1917 and had quickly risen through its ranks. In 1921, he was named Assistant Director of the Bureau. Three years later, Stone named him Director. Hoover would go on to serve for nearly another half century.

**Attorney General
Harlan Fiske Stone**

At the outset, the 29-year-old Hoover was determined to reform the Bureau, quickly and thoroughly, to make it a model of professionalism. He did so by weeding out the "political hacks" and incompetents, laying down a strict code of conduct for agents, and instituting regular inspections of Headquarters and field operations. He insisted on rigorous hiring criteria, including background checks, interviews, and physical tests for all special agent applicants, and in January 1928, he launched the first formal training for incoming agents, a two-month course of instruction and practical exercises in Washington, D.C. Under Hoover's direction, new agents were also required to be 25 to 35 years old, preferably with experience in law or accounting.

When Hoover took over in 1924, the Bureau had about 650 employees, including 441 special agents. In five years, with the rash of firings it had just 339 special agents and less than 600 total employees. But it was beginning to become the organized, professional, and effective force that Hoover envisioned.

One important step in that direction came during Hoover's first year at the helm, when the Bureau was given the responsibility of consolidating the nation's two major collections of fingerprint files (see page 19 for the origins of fingerprinting in the United States). In the summer of 1924, Hoover quickly created an Identification Division (informally called "Ident" in the organization for many years to come) to gather prints from police agencies nationwide and to search them upon request for matches to criminals and crime evidence.

It was a vital new tool for all of law enforcement—the first major building block in Hoover's growing quest to bring the discipline of science to Bureau investigations and scientific services to law enforcement nationwide. Combined with its identification orders, or IOs (see page 7)—early wanted posters that included

Above: The first graduates of the Bureau's training program for national police exectives, the forerunner of today's National Academy, in 1935. Since then, the National Academy has graduated more than 41,000 officers from 166 countries.
Left: A young J. Edgar Hoover

October 11, 1925
First special agent killed in line of duty

New agents train on the rooftop of the Department of Justice building in Washington, D.C., where FBI Headquarters was located from 1933 to 1972

fingerprints and all manner of details about criminal suspects on the run—the Bureau was fast becoming a national hub for crime records. In the late 1920s, the Bureau began exchanging fingerprints with Canada and added more friendly foreign governments in 1932; the following year, it created a corresponding civil fingerprint file for non-criminal cases. By 1936, the agency had a total reservoir of 100,000 fingerprint cards; by 1946, that number had swelled to 100 million.

Using fingerprints to catch the guilty and free the innocent was just the beginning. The lawlessness of the 1920s got the nation's attention, and a number of independent studies—including the Wickersham Commission set up by President Herbert Hoover in

May 1929—confirmed what everyone seemed to already know: that law enforcement at every level needed to modernize.

One glaring need was to get a handle on the national scope of crime by collecting statistics that would enable authorities to understand trends and better focus resources. Taking the lead as it did in many police reforms in the early twentieth century, the International Association of Chiefs of Police created a committee to advance the issue, with Hoover and the Bureau participating. In 1929, the Chiefs adopted a system to classify and report crimes and began to collect crime statistics. The association recommended that the Bureau—with its experience in centralizing criminal records—take the lead. Congress agreed, and the

January 1, 1928
Instituted formal training program for new agents

June 11, 1930
Bureau authorized to collect and compile crime stats

Welcome to the World of Fingerprints

We take it for granted now, but at the turn of the twentieth century the use of fingerprints to identify criminals was still in its infancy.

More popular was the Bertillon system, which measured dozens of features of a criminal's face and body and recorded the series of precise numbers on a large card along with a photograph. After all, the thinking went, what were the chances that two different people would look the same and have identical measurements in all the minute particulars logged by the Bertillon method?

Will West

William West

Not great, of course. But inevitably a case came along to beat the odds.

It happened this way. In 1903, a convicted criminal named Will West was taken to Leavenworth federal prison in Kansas. The clerk at the admissions desk, thinking he recognized West, asked if he'd ever been to Leavenworth. The new prisoner denied it. The clerk took his Bertillon measurements and went to the files, only to return with a card for a "William" West. Turns out, Will and William bore an uncanny resemblance (they may have been identical twins). And their Bertillon measurements were a near match.

The clerk asked Will again if he'd ever been to the prison. "Never," he protested. When the clerk flipped the card over, he discovered Will was telling the truth. "William" was already in Leavenworth, serving a life sentence for murder! Soon after, the fingerprints of both men were taken, and they were clearly different.

It was this incident that caused the Bertillon system to fall "flat on its face," as reporter Don Whitehead aptly put it. The next year, Leavenworth abandoned the method and start fingerprinting its inmates. Thus began the first federal fingerprint collection.

In New York, the state prison had begun fingerprinting its inmates as early as 1903. Following the event at Leavenworth, other police and prison officials followed suit. Leavenworth itself eventually began swapping prints with other agencies, and its collection swelled to more than 800,000 individual records.

By 1920, though, the International Association of Chiefs of

Police had become concerned about the erratic quality and disorganization of criminal identification records in America. It urged the Department of Justice to merge the country's two major fingerprint collections—the federal one at Leavenworth and its own set of state and local ones held in Chicago.

Four years later, a bill was passed providing the funds and giving the task to the young Bureau of Investigation. On July 1, 1924, J. Edgar Hoover, who had been appointed Acting Director less than two months earlier, quickly formed a Division of Identification. He announced that the Bureau would welcome submissions from other jurisdictions and provide identification services to all law enforcement partners. The FBI has done so ever since.

Above: Bureau fingerprint experts at work in 1932
Below: Actual Bertillon measurement cards used to identify criminals before the advent of fingerprints

FEDERAL BUREAU OF INVESTIGATION
UNITED STATES DEPARTMENT OF JUSTICE
J. Edgar Hoover, Director

Bertillon Method of Identification
System of Measurements

Prison Register No. 119   Police Register No. 2150   Anthropometric No.

Name Lawrence Fox   Aliases

Age 25   Year of Birth 1871

Place of Birth Manchester

Complexion Fresh

Hair Brown

Eyes Blue

Occupation Dyer

Sentenced at

Bureau assumed responsibility for the program in 1930. It has been taking this national pulse on crime ever since.

The third major development was a scientific crime lab, long a keen interest of Hoover's. After becoming Director, he had encouraged his agents to keep an eye on advances in science. By 1930, the Bureau was hiring outside experts on a case-by-case basis. Over the next few years, the Bureau's first technical laboratory took root, thanks in large part to a visionary special agent named Charles Appel (page 22). By 1932, the lab was fully operational and soon providing scientific examinations and analysis for the Bureau and its partners around the country.

Charles "Lucky" Luciano

This trio of advances came just in time, as the crime wave that began in the 1920s was about to reach its peak. By the early 1930s, cities like St. Paul, Minnesota, had become virtual training grounds for young crooks, while Hot Springs, Arkansas, had turned into a safe haven and even a vacation spot for the criminal underworld. Al Capone was locked away for good in 1931 (thanks in part to the Bureau, see page 26), but his Chicago Outfit carried on fine without him and would actually experience a resurgence in the coming decades. The "Five Families" of the New York Mafia were also emerging during this period, with "Lucky" Luciano setting up the "Commission" to unite the mob and "Murder, Inc." to carry out its hits. Prohibition was ultimately repealed in 1933, but by then, the Great Depression was in full force, and with honest jobs harder to come by than ever, the dishonest ones sometimes seemed more attractive than standing in soup lines.

By 1933, an assortment of dangerous and criminally prolific gangsters was wreaking havoc across America, especially in the Midwest. Their names would soon be known far and wide.

There was John Dillinger, with his crooked smile, who managed to charm the press and much of America into believing he

Employees of the "Ident" division in 1929. The Bureau began managing the nation's fingerprint collections five years earlier.

The Birth of the FBI Lab

In the pages of FBI history, November 24, 1932, is considered the official birthday of the FBI Laboratory. But it is really a "declared" anniversary for what was an evolving concept.

From the 1920s on, Director Hoover had been actively interested in scientific analysis, and by 1930 he had authorized the use of outside experts on a case-by-case basis in identification and evidence examination matters. Then, over a two-year period, the first true "technical" laboratory functions began to

**Special Agent
Charles Appel**

take shape. When all these functions moved into Room 802 of the Old Southern Railway Building in Washington, D.C., it seemed appropriate to recognize that a true lab had been born.

It was Special Agent Charles Appel who was its midwife. He had served as an aviator in World War I before joining the Bureau in 1924—and right from the start he focused on meticulous investigations based on scientific detection.

Appel was an extraordinary man with extraordinary vision, fully backed by Director Hoover with the necessary resources. He took courses to further his knowledge of state-of-the-art techniques, and by 1931, he began seeking expert opinion on starting a crime lab. In July 1932, when he proposed "a separate division for the handling of so-called crime prevention work" under which "the crimino-

The FBI Laboratory's first home: Room 802 of the Old Southern Railway Building in Washington, D.C.

logical research laboratory could be placed," he got an immediate endorsement. By September, Room 802 in the Old Southern Railway building was fully equipped. By November 24, it was in business.

The new lab was pretty sophisticated by 1932 standards. It included a brand new ultra-violet light machine; a microscope, on loan from Bausch and Lomb until the requisition for its purchase could be finalized; moulage kits (for taking impressions); photographic supplies; and chemical sets. A machine to examine the interior of gun barrels was on order.

For about a year, Appel was the Bureau's one-man lab. His handwriting and typewriter font analysis solved a poisoning case in 1933. His analysis of handwriting on the Lindbergh kidnapping ransom notes ultimately helped convict Bruno Richard Hauptmann (see page 27).

Agents across the Bureau soon started receiving training on what this new lab could do for them and their cases, and they spread the word about the value of scientific work to their law enforcement partners.

By January 1940, the lab had a total of 46 employees. As America headed into a second world war, its growing skills and capabilities would be needed more than ever.

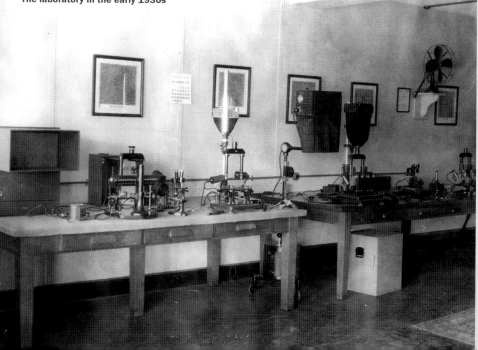

The laboratory in the early 1930s

was nothing more than a harmless, modern-day Robin Hood. In reality, Dillinger and his revolving crew of gunslingers—violent thugs like Homer Van Meter, Harry "Pete" Pierpont, and John "Red" Hamilton—were shooting up banks across America's heartland, stealing hundreds of thousands of dollars and murdering at least one policeman along the way.

There was Clyde Barrow and his girlfriend Bonnie Parker, an inseparable, love-struck couple who—partnered at times with the Barrow brothers and others—were robbing and murdering their way across a half dozen or so states.

There was the ruthless, almost psychopathic "Baby Face" Nelson, who worked with everyone from Roger "The Terrible" Touhy to Al Capone and Dillinger over the course of his crime career and teamed up with John Paul Chase and Fatso Negri in his latter days. Nelson was a callous killer who thought nothing of murdering lawmen; he gunned down three Bureau agents,

for instance, in the span of seven months. And there was the cunning Alvin Karpis and his Barker brother sidekicks, who not only robbed banks and trains but engineered two major kidnappings of rich Minnesota business executives in 1933.

All of these criminals would become "public enemies," actively hunted by law enforcement nationwide. At first, the Bureau was playing only a bit part in pursuing these gangsters, since few of their crimes violated federal laws. But that began to change with the 1932 Lindbergh kidnapping (see page 27), which gave the Bureau jurisdiction in these cases for the first time; with the "Kansas City Massacre" in June 1933 (see page 28), a bloody slaughter at a train station that claimed the lives of four lawmen, including a Bureau agent; and with the rise to national prominence of John Dillinger.

Using whatever federal laws it could hang its hat on, the Bureau turned its full attention to catching these gangsters. And

The rising popularity of the FBI's "G-men" (see page 24) spawned hundreds of toys and games.

November 24, 1932
Bureau launches a Technical Crime Lab

September 26, 1933
"Machine Gun" Kelly reportedly coins "G-Men" nickname

June 18, 1934
Legislation passed giving new jurisdiction and tools to Bureau

"Machine Gun" Kelly and the Legend of the G-Men

Before 1934, "G-Man" was underworld slang for any and all government agents. In fact, the detectives in J. Edgar Hoover's Bureau of Investigation were so little known that they were often confused with Secret Service or Prohibition Bureau agents. By 1935, though, only one kind of government employee was known by that name, the special agents of the Bureau.

George "Machine Gun" Kelly

How this change came about is not entirely clear, but September 26, 1933, played a central role in the apocryphal origins of this change.

On that day, Bureau of Investigation agents and Tennessee police officers arrested gangster George "Machine Gun" Kelly. He was a "wanted fugitive" for good reason. Two months earlier Kelly had kidnapped oil magnate Charles Urschel and held him for $200,000 in ransom. After Urschel was released, the Bureau coordinated a multi-state investigation, drawing investigative information from its own field offices as well as from other police sources, as it identified and then tracked the notorious gangster across the country.

On September 26, "Machine Gun" Kelly was found hiding in a decrepit Memphis residence. Some early press reports said that a tired, perhaps hung-over Kelly stumbled out of his bed mumbling something like "I was expecting you." Another version of the event held that Kelly emerged from his room, hands-up, crying "Don't shoot G-Men, don't shoot." Either way, Kelly was arrested without violence.

The rest is history. The more colorful version sparked the popular imagination and "G-Men" became synonymous with the special agents of the FBI.

despite some stumbles along the way, the successes began to add up. By the end of 1934, most of these public enemies had been killed or captured.

"Doc" Barker

Bonnie and Clyde were the first to fall, in May 1934, at the hands of Texas lawmen (with the Bureau playing a small supporting role in tracking them down—see page 29). In July, Melvin Purvis and a team of agents caught up with Dillinger, who was shot dead leaving a Chicago theater (see page 30). "Pretty Boy" Floyd, one of the hired hands of the Kansas City Massacre, was killed in a shootout with Bureau agents and local law enforcement on an Ohio farm in October 1934. And Nelson died the following month after a bloody firefight with two special agents, who were also killed.

Kate "Ma" Barker

The Bureau caught up with the rest soon enough. Agents arrested "Doc" Barker in January 1935, and the infamous "Ma" Barker and her son Fred were killed by Bureau agents in Florida eight days later (see pictures on page 25). Alvin Karpis, the brains of the gang, was captured in May 1936 and ended up in Alcatraz.

Alvin Karpis

In just a few transformative years, thanks to the successful battle against gangsters, the once unknown Bureau and its "G-Men" (see inset) became household names and icons of popular culture. Along the way, Congress had given it newfound powers, too, including the ability to carry guns and make arrests. In July 1935, as the capstone of its newfound identity, the organization was renamed the Federal Bureau of Investigation—the FBI.

As the decade came to a close, the FBI would find itself shifting gears once again. War was brewing in Europe, and pro-Nazi groups were becoming more and more vocal in the U.S., claiming fascism was the answer to American woes. The gangsters, it turned out, were just a prelude to the dark days to come.

July 22, 1934
Dillinger killed by Bureau agents

Above: The Florida home (right) where
"Doc" and "Ma" Barker were killed in a
shootout with Bureau agents
Right: The cache of Barker weapons recovered
by agents after the firefight

July 1, 1935
Organization re-named Federal Bureau of Investigation

July 29, 1935
FBI creates the National Academy, its first national police training program

FAMOUS CASES

Solving Scarface: How the Law Caught Up with Al Capone

In the "Roaring Twenties," he ruled an empire of crime in the Windy City: gambling, prostitution, bootlegging, bribery, narcotics trafficking, robbery, protection rackets, and murder. And it seemed that law enforcement couldn't touch him.

The early Bureau would have been happy to join the fight to take Capone down. But it needed a federal crime to hang its case on—and the evidence to back it up.

In those days, racketeering laws weren't what they are today. Even when it was widely rumored that Capone had ordered the brutal murders of seven gangland rivals in the infamous "St. Valentine's Day Massacre," the Bureau couldn't get involved. Why? The killings weren't a federal offense.

Then, in 1929, the Bureau got a break.

On February 27, Capone was subpoenaed at his winter home near Miami, Florida, to appear as a witness before a federal grand jury in Chicago on March 12 for a case involving a violation of prohibition laws.

Capone said he couldn't make it. His excuse? He claimed he'd been laid up with broncho-pneumonia for six weeks and was in no shape to travel. And he had the doctor's note to "prove it."

That's when the Bureau got involved. Asked by the U.S. Attorney in Chicago to find out whether Capone was on the level, agents went to Florida and quickly found that Capone's story didn't hold water. When he was supposedly bedridden, Capone was out and about—going to the racetracks, taking trips to the Bahamas, even being questioned by local prosecutors. And by all accounts, his health was just fine.

On March 27, 1929, Capone was cited for contempt of court in Chicago and arrested in Florida. He was released on bond, but from then on, it was downhill for the notorious gangster. Less than two months later, Capone was arrested in Philadelphia by local police for carrying concealed weapons and was sent to jail for a year. When he was released in 1931, Capone was tried and convicted for the original contempt of court charge. A federal judge sentenced him to six months in prison. His air of invincibility was fast slipping away.

In the meantime, federal Treasury agents had been gathering evidence that Capone had failed to pay his income taxes. Capone was convicted, and on October 24, 1931, he was sentenced to 11 years in prison. When he finally got out of Alcatraz, Capone was too sick to carry on his life of crime. He died in 1947.

In the end, it took a team of federal, state, and local authorities—and a lot of grit and persistence—to end Capone's reign as underworld boss.

Al Capone's criminal record and fingerprint card

FAMOUS CASES

The Lindbergh Kidnapping

On a beautiful 390-acre estate on the rural outskirts of Hopewell, New Jersey, Charles Lindbergh and his wife Anne hoped to stay out of the constant glare of the media spotlight in the years following the aviator's historic non-stop flight across the Atlantic.

Charles Lindbergh

It was not to be. On March 1, 1932, a crime took place that stunned the nation and made the Lindberghs and their ensuing tragedy front-page news for months to come.

It happened quickly and without warning. At around 9 p.m., the couple's 20-month old son was sleeping in his nursery on the second floor when someone leaned a ladder against the house, climbed through a window, and made off with the boy. The kidnapping was discovered about an hour later, along with a ransom note demanding $50,000.

Bruno Richard Hauptmann

A massive investigation was launched, led by the New Jersey State Police. A dozen more ransom notes followed, including one that led to a meeting where Dr. John Condon, representing the Lindbergh family, paid a mysterious man named "John" $50,000 in gold certificates for the safe return of the child. But on May 12, 1932, the boy's body was discovered less than five miles from the Lindbergh home. The boy had apparently been killed by a blow to the head shortly after the kidnapping.

The Bureau was involved in the case almost from the beginning, offering any and all help to the New Jersey State Police. In the early days of the case, kidnapping was not a federal crime. A day after the boy's remains were found, though, President Herbert Hoover ordered all national investigative agencies to help state authorities, with the Bureau taking the federal lead.

In the coming months, the Bureau left no investigative stone unturned. Agents followed thousands of leads, including a number of bogus reports that spawned cases of their own. Working with Dr. Condon and others, the Bureau developed a likeness of "John" and a profile of his character and education. And through its new scientific crime lab in Washington, the Bureau carefully studied the handwriting in the ransom notes, concluding the author was German.

A break in the case came from the ransom money. On May 2, 1933, nearly 300 gold certificates matching the ransom money were reported as deposited, but no useful information was uncovered from this lead. On August 20, 1934, 16 more certificates were found, and through painstaking investigative legwork investigators closed in on an area in New York City where the bills were circulating and developed a description of the suspect, which closely resembled the portrait of "John."

Less than a month later, a 10-dollar ransom certificate was traced to a gas station, where an alert attendant had written down the license plate of a car used by the man who had cashed the money. The license was traced to Bruno Richard Hauptmann, a German carpenter living in the Bronx. He was arrested on September 19, 1934.

The evidence pointed to Hauptmann as the culprit. He had more ransom money in his home. His handwriting matched that on the ransom notes. His car was similar to one sighted near the Lindbergh home. His tools were matched to tool marks on the ladder at the crime scene. In the end, he was convicted and sentenced to death.

For the Bureau, the case was a significant one. It demonstrated its growing scientific approach to solving crimes and was one of the earliest success stories of its new crime lab. And in response to the tragedy, Congress put the Bureau in the business of solving kidnappings, which it has been doing ever since.

Left: Charles Lindbergh Jr., who was kidnapped and murdered in 1932

Top: The artist sketches of "John" closely resembled Hauptmann
Bottom: Hauptmann's first ransom note, left on the window sill the evening of the kidnapping

FAMOUS CASES

The Kansas City Massacre

The sun rose on June 17, 1933, just like any other spring day in America's heartland. But outside a massive train station in Kansas City, Missouri, a grand tragedy was about to unfold.

Shortly after 7 a.m., a sudden burst of gunfire erupted outside the east entrance of Union Station. Its target was a troupe of lawmen who had just loaded escaped bank robber Frank "Jelly" Nash into a two-door Chevrolet, preparing to return him to the nearby Leavenworth prison.

Within seconds, two Kansas City police officers, an Oklahoma police chief named Otto Reed, and Bureau Special Agent Ray Caffrey had been murdered—along with Nash himself. Another two agents inside the car survived by slumping forward and pretending to be dead. Kansas City Special Agent in Charge Reed Vetterli, who had been standing near the front of the car, miraculously escaped with only a flesh wound. An officer who responded from inside the station fired at the escaping killers, but they got away.

This brazen slaughter by submachine gun came to be called "The Kansas City Massacre," and it turned into one of the early Bureau's most important investigations, leading to a massive manhunt for the culprits and ultimately helping the agency gain new law enforcement powers.

Who did it and why? That's what the Bureau aimed to find out. It was tough going in the early days, with few solid leads and the recollections of surviving lawmen and witnesses less than clear.

Ultimately, the evidence pointed to a bank robber and underworld assassin named Verne Miller as the leader of the plot. Miller was a good friend of Nash, and Nash's wife had apparently contacted the gunman to help spring her husband after he was arrested the day before the massacre.

Miller raced to Kansas City, but he realized he needed help to free his friend. There, he was apparently introduced to Charles "Pretty Boy" Floyd, a notorious

bank robber on the run, and his confederate Adam Richetti. It was these three men, the Bureau concluded, who had carried out the crime.

The first priority was to find Miller. In October, agents traced him to the apartment of his girlfriend Vivian Mathias in Chicago. Miller escaped, but Mathias was captured and later pled guilty to harboring the fugitive. A month later, on November 29, the search came to an end when Miller turned up dead in a ditch near Detroit, Michigan, a victim of a dispute with the New Jersey underworld.

Bureau agents then turned their full attention to finding Floyd and Richetti. The two men, they learned, had been traveling with a pair of women. On October 20, 1934, the four were driving in Ohio when Floyd crashed into a telephone pole. While the women took the car into the nearby town of Wellsville for repairs, Richetti and Floyd were spotted by local police and ended up in a firefight. Richetti was quickly captured, but Floyd got away. Two days later, Bureau agents and local authorities tracked Floyd to a farm near Clarkson, Ohio, where he was shot and killed.

The Kansas City Massacre was a dark chapter for law enforcement and for the FBI in particular—at that time, one of the deadliest attacks on the law the nation had ever seen. Within a year of the tragedy, Congress responded by giving Bureau agents new tools to fight crime—including statutory authority to carry guns and make arrests, both of which have been pillars in the FBI's work to protect the nation ever since.

Frank "Jelly" Nash

**Special Agent
Ray Caffrey**

**Special Agent in Charge
Reed Vetterli**

**Scene in front of the Kansas City railroad depot
moments after the attack**

FAMOUS CASES

Bonnie and Clyde

She was just shy of five feet tall, all of 90 pounds, a part-time waitress and amateur poet from a poor Dallas home who was bored with life and wanted something more.

He was a fast-talking, small-time thief from a similarly destitute Dallas family who hated poverty and wanted to make a name for himself.

Together, they became the most notorious crime couple in American history—Bonnie and Clyde.

Their story, though romanticized on the silver screen, was hardly a glamorous one. From the summer of 1932 until the spring of 1934, they left a trail of violence and terror in their wake as they crisscrossed the countryside in a series of stolen cars, robbing gas stations, village groceries, and the occasional bank and taking hostages when they got into a tight spot. Clyde was good with a gun and didn't hesitate to use it, allegedly murdering at least a dozen people, including police and innocent bystanders alike. Bonnie wasn't just along for the ride. Though she probably never fired a shot, she was his willing accomplice.

Bonnie Parker and Clyde Barrow had met in Texas in January 1930 and by most accounts were immediately smitten with each other. They were just kids. Barrow, already an ex-con, was a few months short of 21. Parker, already an ex-wife (though not officially divorced), was just 19.

Clyde was arrested a few days after they met, but Bonnie helped him escape by smuggling a gun into his Waco jail. They robbed their way across the Midwest, until Clyde was captured and thrown in jail once more. He was paroled in early 1932 and soon returned to a life of crime, apparently murdering an Oklahoma sheriff and storekeeper. By August, Bonnie and Clyde were together for good and making news, and they were pursued across Texas, Oklahoma, Missouri, Louisiana, Arkansas, Kansas, Iowa, and Illinois.

The Bureau joined the chase in 1933. Until then, it lacked the jurisdiction to get involved in what were local crimes. But in the spring of that year agents gathered evidence from a stolen car that had crossed state lines—and traced it to the elusive pair. That led to federal interstate car theft charges and enabled the Bureau to officially join the manhunt in May 1933.

At that point, Bureau agents went to work, distributing wanted notices with fingerprints, photographs, descriptions, criminal records, and other information to police officers across the country. Agents followed the couple's trail through many states and into their various haunts, particularly in Louisiana. Bureau agents discovered the couple's association with Henry Methvin and the Methvin family of Louisiana, and they found that Bonnie and Clyde had been driving a car stolen in New Orleans. The Methvins ultimately decided to help authorities locate the couple.

The end came on May 23, 1934. Police officers from Louisiana and Texas, including Texas Ranger Frank Hamer, hid in the bushes along a dirt road near Gibsland, Louisiana. Around nine in the morning, Bonnie and Clyde drove up in their tan Ford. They slowed down when they came across Henry Methvin's father Ivy standing beside his truck as if it was broken down. It was a trap. Ivy ducked away, and the officers opened fire. Bonnie and Clyde were killed instantly.

In the end, Bonnie and Clyde died as they lived—in a hail of bullets. Their murderous days were over, but the legend of Bonnie and Clyde—often rooted more in fiction than in fact—would only grow in the years to come.

Bonnie and Clyde, who liked taking pictures of themselves, posing for the camera. Below are their actual "Identification Orders" (wanted posters) issued by the Bureau.

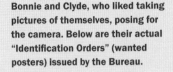

IDENTIFICATION ORDER NO. 1227
May 21, 1934.

DIVISION OF INVEST
U. S. DEPARTMENT OF
WASHINGTON, D

WANTED

MRS. ROY THORNTON, aliases BONNIE BARROW,
MRS. CLYDE BARROW, BONNIE PARKER.

NATIONAL MOTOR
VEHICLE THEFT ACT

DESCRIPTION

Age, 23 years (1933); Height, 5 feet, 5 inches; Weight, 100 pounds; Build, slender; Hair, auburn, bobbed; originally blonde; Eyes, blue; Complexion, fair; Scars and marks, bullet wound left foot next to little toe; bullet in left knee; burn scar on right leg from hip to knee; Peculiarities, walks with both knees slightly buckled.

RELATIVES

Roy Thornton, husba
State Penitentia
Mrs. J. T. (Emma) P
South Lamar St.,
Mrs. Billie Parker
South Lamar St.,
Hubert (Buster) Par
Gladewater, Texa
Nellie Gonzales, h
Gonzales County

CRIMINAL

Arrested sheriff'
Texas, June 16,
burglary; rele

IDENTIFICATION ORDER NO. 1211
October 24, 1933

DIVIS
U. S.

WANTED

CLYDE CHAMPION BARROW, aliases CLYDE BARROW, E
WILLIAMS, ELDIN WILLIAMS, JACK HALE, ROY BAILEY.

Clyde Champio

FAMOUS CASES

The Fall of John Dillinger

The movie playing at the Biograph Theater on this hot, muggy summer night was *Manhattan Melodrama*, starring Clark Gable as the ruthless gangster Blackie Gallagher.

But it was the real-life drama starring notorious outlaw John Dillinger that was playing out on the streets of Chicago on this particular Sunday evening that would ultimately captivate the nation and forever transform the FBI.

It was July 22, 1934. A nervous Melvin Purvis, Special Agent in Charge of the Bureau's office in Chicago, stood near the Biograph box office. He'd seen Dillinger walk into the crowded theater about two hours earlier with two women, including one in an orange skirt (often called a "red dress") who had tipped off authorities that the wanted criminal would be there. Now, Purvis waited for Dillinger to re-emerge.

Special Agent in Charge Melvin Purvis

Suddenly, Purvis saw him. Purvis took out a match and lit his cigar. It was a pre-arranged signal to the Bureau agents and local police officers taking part in the operation, but in the thick crowd less than a half-dozen of the men saw it.

People pose in front of the Biograph Theater shortly after John Dillinger's death. One woman is holding a newspaper with the headline, "Dillinger Slain."

In the preceding year, many such opportunities to catch the wanted outlaw and other gangsters had gone up in smoke, enhancing Dillinger's legend. The Bureau had learned many lessons, often the hard way, in the process. Three months earlier, a special agent had been gunned down following a hastily planned raid on a Dillinger gang hideout in Wisconsin. And 13 months earlier, the Bureau had lost an agent and three law enforcement partners at the hands of "Pretty Boy" Floyd and others in the infamous "Kansas City Massacre."

But on this night, the Bureau was prepared. The arrangement of agents, the setting of the signal, and the careful preparation were evidence that it was learning how to catch the most violent criminals. The plan was not perfect, but it was sound, with agents covering all theater exits and directions Dillinger might take.

As Dillinger walked down the street, agents fell in behind him and closed in. Dillinger sensed something was wrong, and as Special Agent Charles Winstead would later describe, the gangster "whirled around and reached for his right front pocket [where he had a .380 Colt automatic pistol]. He started running sideways toward the alley."

Agents fired. Dillinger fell, mumbled a few words, and died.

The manhunt was over. It was the beginning of the end of the gangster era and a cornerstone in the evolution of the Bureau.

John Dillinger's Colt .380

FAMOUS CASES

The Final Hours of "Baby Face" Nelson

He was a protégé of Alvin Karpis and a partner of John Dillinger.

But Lester Gillis, better known by his alias George "Baby Face" Nelson, was far too ruthless and reckless for even those hardened gangsters. Despite his boyish looks (thus the nickname), Nelson was a callous killer with a violent temper. He killed three Bureau agents, more than anyone in history. Eventually even Dillinger refused to rob banks with him.

Helen Gillis

The Bureau's search for Nelson intensified after Dillinger's death in July 1934. By late November, agents were closing in. Here's the story of the outlaw's last hours and the ultimate price paid by the two agents who ended his violent career.

John Paul Chase

November 27, 2:00 p.m.: Two Bureau agents on a stakeout in Lake Geneva, Wisconsin (about 60 miles northwest of Chicago), encountered Nelson. Nelson fled but was later spotted nearby by another agent, who got his license plate number. With Nelson were his wife, Helen Gillis, and John Paul Chase, Nelson's long-time partner.

Special Agent Samuel P. Cowley

Around 2:45 p.m.: Samuel P. Cowley, the Bureau inspector spearheading the search for Nelson, learned that "Baby Face" may be heading towards Chicago. Cowley immediately sent Agents Bill Ryan and Tom McDade out to look for Nelson's car on the highway. He then grabbed Agent Herman "Ed" Hollis and headed out in a second car.

Circa 3:15 p.m.: Agents Ryan and McDade noticed Nelson heading south on the highway; they made a u-turn and pursued him. Nelson saw them and made two u-turns of his own so that he was now following the agents. A firefight began. Agent Ryan pierced the radiator of Nelson's car, and it started to sputter.

Moments later: Agents Cowley and Hollis passed Nelson and

his partners who are sputtering down the highway. Hollis made a u-turn and followed. His car disabled, Nelson pulled off the road near a park in Barrington, Illinois. Nelson and Chase got out and took up positions with their weapons. Hollis skidded to a stop about 150 feet past the outlaw's car. Chase and Nelson immediately opened fire. Both agents jumped out of their car and returned fire. Hollis was killed, Cowley mortally wounded. Nelson was hurt badly as well, with 17 gunshot wounds, but he was able to get in the Bureau car with his partners and speed off.

Around 8:00 p.m.: Nelson died in Wilmette, Illinois, 16 miles north of downtown Chicago.

November 28, 2:17 a.m.: Inspector Cowley died.

Circa 12:30 p.m.: Acting on a tip, police found Nelson's body in a ditch near a cemetery.

Post Script: Both Chase and Helen Gillis were caught within the month and sent to jail, closing the chapter on the Nelson gang.

Above: Nelson's mug shot
Below: The Bureau's Identification Order for Lester M. Gillis, aka "Baby Face" Nelson

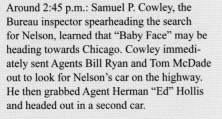

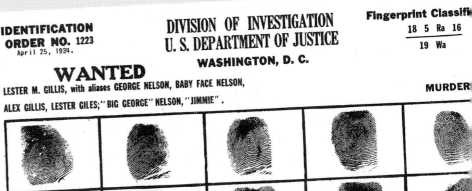

IDENTIFICATION ORDER NO. 1223
April 25, 1934.

DIVISION OF INVESTIGATION
U. S. DEPARTMENT OF JUSTICE
WASHINGTON, D. C.

Fingerprint Classifi
18 5 Ra 16
19 Wa

WANTED

LESTER M. GILLIS, with aliases GEORGE NELSON, BABY FACE NELSON, ALEX GILLIS, LESTER GILES; "BIG GEORGE" NELSON, "JIMMIE".

MURDER

World War, Cold War, *1939 to 1953*

Heading into the late 1930s, fresh off a victory over the gun-slinging gangsters, the FBI hardly had time to catch its collective breath.

The Bureau had reformed itself on the fly; it was stronger and more capable than ever. But now, with the world rushing headlong into war and the pendulum swinging back towards national security concerns, the FBI would need to refocus and retool its operations once again.

At the start of the decade, the public enemies were almost entirely homegrown—from "Scarface" to "Baby Face." The next wave of villains would come primarily from afar, and they were in many respects bigger and badder still. They were hyper-aggressive fascist dictators, fanatical militarists, and revolution-exporting communists—along with their legions of spies, saboteurs, and subversive agents—who sought to invade, infiltrate, or even conquer entire swaths of territory, if not the world. They threatened not only the fate of peoples and nations, but the survival of democracy itself.

Across the Atlantic in Europe, 1939 was a dark turning point. Five years earlier, less than a month after a cornered Dillinger had reached for his gun the last time, a power-hungry Adolph Hitler had declared himself "Führer" and taken total control of Germany. Hitler wasted little time rearming the country. He meant to build an empire—the Third Reich—and within a few years he'd annexed Austria and the Sudetenland, a German-speaking region in Czechoslovakia. England and France, hoping to cut their losses through appeasement, acceded to the take-overs. But in 1939, Hitler seized the rest of the Czechoslovakia and invaded Poland. England and France had seen enough and declared war.

Dueling dictators: Hitler and Mussolini in 1940

In the Far East, Japan was making military waves as well. It invaded China in 1937, seized its northern capital, began taking

control of coastal areas and nearby islands dotting the Pacific, and even deliberately sank an American gunboat. It formally joined with Germany and Mussolini's Italy to form the Axis powers in September 1940.

June 24, 1940
Special Intelligence Service established

Dark days: A mass roll call of Nazi troops in Nuremberg, November 9, 1935

Members of the German American Bund parade through the streets of New York. Anastase Vonsiatsky (far left) pled guilty to espionage in 1942.

Cushioned by twin oceans, an isolationist America was staying out of the fray—for the time being. But, remembering how helpless it was against German sabotage in the years leading up to World War I, the nation wasn't taking any chances at home. The lingering Great Depression provided fertile ground for fascism. Groups like the German American Bund and the Silver Shirts that embraced the Nazi vision were becoming more and more vocal. And Americans were increasingly becoming enamored of communism and its seductive promise of a classless state; the Communist Party of the United States and other like-minded organizations soon boasted more than a million members.

President Roosevelt was concerned—he suspected these groups were allying themselves to foreign political movements seeking to overturn democracy and were crossing the line into criminal activity. In 1934, he had first asked the FBI to determine if American Nazi groups were working with foreign agents. In 1936, the President and Secretary of State tasked the Bureau with gathering intelligence on the potential threats to national security posed by fascist and communist groups.

Meanwhile, Nazi espionage on U.S. soil had become a real

threat. The intelligence arms of the Army and Navy had noticed increased activity by German and Japanese spies in the late 1930s and began working with the Bureau to disrupt it. Learning the counterintelligence ropes as it went along, the FBI was ultimately given the lead in these cases and uncovered some 50 spies operating in America before the nation entered the war, including a massive ring led by long-time German agent Fritz Duquesne (see page 44).

As the new decade opened, the nation was drifting towards war and increasingly supporting the Allied cause. It clearly needed more and better intelligence to understand the threats posed by the Axis powers. The Bureau had been put in charge of domestic intelligence and had already built an extensive network of sources, with law enforcement around the country serving as an important set of eyes and ears. It had also begun developing connections abroad with Canadian and British intelligence and law enforcement.

But who would handle overseas intelligence? There was no CIA in 1940—and its predecessor, the Office of Strategic Services, would not be launched until June 1942. Roosevelt decided to

The Special Intelligence Service

Who was the "golfer" who easily won a local championship overseas and went on to become personal friends with the country's political leaders?

Who was the "traveling companion" of a South American police official—an official who boasted that he "could spot any FBI undercover man on sight"?

Who was the "visitor" to a foreign country who drew up legislation that improved that nation's ability to protect itself against Axis intelligence activities?

They were all FBI agents, working undercover in Central and South America during World War II as part of the Bureau's "Special Intelligence Service," established in 1940 as a response to an order of President Roosevelt.

It was a vital mission. By 1940, South America had become a hotbed of German intrigue. More than half-a-million German emigrants—many supporters of the Third Reich—had settled in Brazil and Argentina alone. In line with the Bureau's earlier intelligence work on threats posed by Germany, Roosevelt wanted to keep an eye on Nazi activities in our neighbors to the south. And when the U.S. joined the Allied cause in 1941, the President wanted to protect the nation from Hitler's spies and collect intelligence on Axis activities to help win the war.

Over the next seven years, the FBI sent more than 340 agents and support professionals undercover into Central and South America as part of the Special Intelligence Service.

There was a significant learning curve—it took some time for the FBI to get undercover operatives in place and to master the languages. But within months, the Special Intelligence Service was working well. The service was gathering information and sending it back to FBI Headquarters in Washington, where it was crafted into useful intelligence for the military and others. And overseas, it developed ways of sharing crucial information with law enforcement and intelligence services there so they could round up Axis spies and saboteurs.

How successful was the Special Intelligence Service? The numbers speak for themselves. By 1946, it had identified 887 Axis spies, 281 propaganda agents, 222 agents smuggling strategic war materials, 30 saboteurs, and 97 other agents. It had located 24 secret Axis radio stations and confiscated 40 radio transmitters and 18 receiving sets. And the FBI had even used some of these radio networks to pass false and misleading information back to Nazi Germany.

The Special Intelligence Service was disbanded after the war, and the newly formed CIA was asked to take over its operations and expand U.S. intelligence activities worldwide. But the intelligence operation served the nation well: it helped protect the homeland, provided valuable lessons in intelligence and undercover operations for the Bureau for years to come, and set the stage for the FBI's overseas Legal Attaché program.

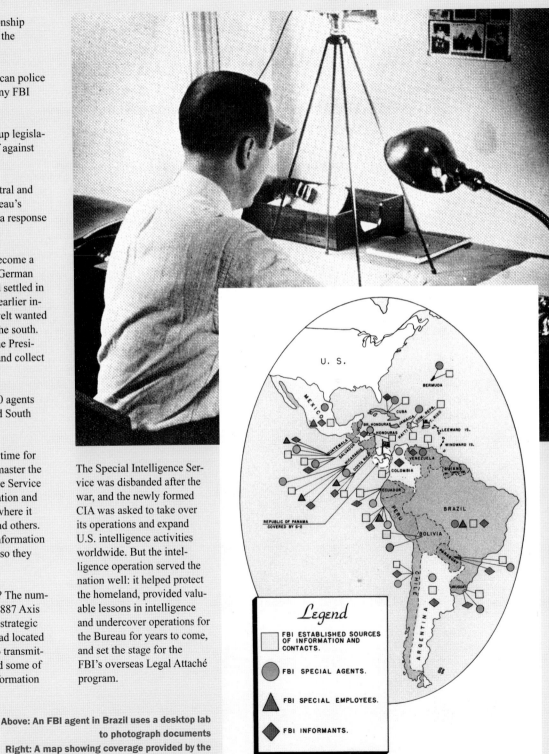

Above: An FBI agent in Brazil uses a desktop lab to photograph documents
Right: A map showing coverage provided by the Special Intelligence Service in the Western Hemisphere

Legend

FBI ESTABLISHED SOURCES OF INFORMATION AND CONTACTS.

FBI SPECIAL AGENTS.

FBI SPECIAL EMPLOYEES.

FBI INFORMANTS.

assign intelligence responsibilities for different parts of the globe to various agencies. The Bureau landed the area closest to home—the Western Hemisphere.

Strategically, it made sense—South and Central America were fast becoming staging grounds for the Nazis to send spies into the U.S. and hubs for relaying information back to Germany. In one of the least well known success stories in Bureau history, the FBI responded to the President's charge by setting up a Special Intelligence Service in June 1940 that sent scores of agents undercover to knock out the Axis spy nests (see page 35). Around that time, it also started officially stationing agents as diplomatic liaisons in U.S. embassies—the forerunner of today's

Legal Attachés—to coordinate international leads arising from the Bureau's work.

When war finally did come to America—with a bang at Pearl Harbor—the Bureau was ready. In fact, as the bombs fell, Honolulu Special Agent in Charge Robert Shivers was on the phone with FBI Headquarters and Director Hoover, who quickly implemented the war plans the FBI already had in place and put the organization on a 24/7 schedule.

One important step the Bureau had taken in the run-up to war was to put together a list of German, Italian, and Japanese aliens in the U.S. who posed a clear threat to the country. Under presidential order issued on the evening of December 7, the Bureau moved to arrest these enemies and present them to immigration officials for hearings (represented by counsel) and for possible deportation. Within 72 hours, more than 3,800 aliens had been taken into custody without incident.

Remembering the civil rights lessons of the "Palmer Raids" (see page 12) in 1920, Hoover wanted nothing to do with the hysteria that called for rounding up Japanese-Americans on a much wider scale. He opposed that step, arguing that the Bureau had already moved against the real threats. But fear and prejudice prevailed, and in early 1942, some 120,000 Japanese—more than half U.S. citizens—were hastily detained and interred by the military under executive order.

For the FBI, life during wartime was incredibly busy. The Bureau had a vital role to play in protecting the homeland and supporting the war effort—from rounding up draft dodgers to investigating companies that deliberately supplied defective war materials just to turn a tidier profit. The FBI continued performing background checks on federal workers to keep criminals from entering the government. It kept working to head off espionage and stepped up its efforts to gather and analyze intelligence and to feed it to policymakers. The FBI Laboratory, growing stronger and more capable by the year, played a pioneering role by helping to break enemy codes and by engineering sophisticated intercepts.

The FBI was also in charge of preventing sabotage at home, and that meant running to ground every hint and rumor of potential attack. None of the reports the Bureau received and investigated—more than 20,000 in all—ultimately panned out; not a single act of enemy-directed sabotage was carried out on U.S. soil during the conflict. But that was hardly an accident. Before the country had entered the war, the FBI had surveyed more than 2,000 major industrial plants in the country and provided a series of suggestions on tightening their security, including lessons agents learned from the British.

That didn't mean the Nazis didn't try to attack the homeland

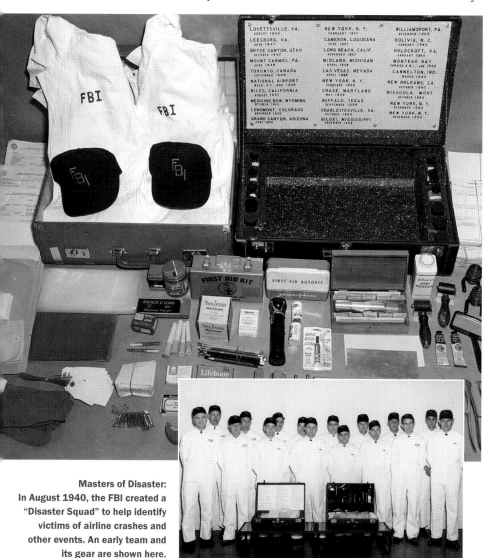

Masters of Disaster: In August 1940, the FBI created a "Disaster Squad" to help identify victims of airline crashes and other events. An early team and its gear are shown here.

The Case of the Treasonous Dolls

In early 1942, five letters were written and mailed by seemingly different people in different U.S. locations to the same person at an address in Buenos Aires, Argentina. Even more strangely, all of them bounced "Return to Sender"—and the "senders" on the return address (women in Oregon, Ohio, Colorado, and Washington state) knew nothing about the letters and had not sent them.

The FBI learned about all this when wartime censors intercepted one letter postmarked in Portland, Oregon, puzzled over its strange contents, and referred it to cryptographers at the FBI Laboratory. These experts concluded that the three "Old English dolls" left at "a wonderful doll hospital" for repairs might well mean three warships being repaired at a west coast naval shipyard; that "fish nets" meant submarine nets; and that "balloons" referred to defense installations.

Velvalee Malvena Dickinson

The FBI immediately opened an investigation.

It was May 20, 1942, when a woman in Seattle turned over the crucial second letter. It said, "The wife of an important business associate gave her an old German bisque Doll dressed in a Hulu Grass skirt...I broke this awful doll...I walked all over Seattle to get someone to repair it...."

In short order, the FBI turned up the other letters. It determined that all five were using "doll code" to describe vital information about U.S. naval matters. All had forged signatures that had been made from authentic original signatures. All had typing characteristics that showed they were typed by the same person on different typewriters. How to put these clues together?

It was the woman in Colorado who provided the big break. She, like the other purported letter senders, was a doll collector, and she believed that a Madison Avenue doll shop owner, Mrs. Velvalee Dickinson, was responsible. She said Ms. Dickinson was angry with her because she'd been late paying for some dolls she'd ordered. That name was a match: the other women were also her customers.

Who was Velvalee Malvena Dickinson? Basically, a mystery. She was born in California and lived there until she moved with her husband to New York City in 1937. She opened a doll shop on Madison Avenue that same year, catering to wealthy doll collectors and hobbyists, but she struggled to keep it afloat. It also turned out that she had a long and close association with the Japanese diplomatic mission in the U.S.—and she had $13,000 in her safe deposit box traceable to Japanese sources.

Following her guilty plea on July 28, 1944, Ms. Dickinson detailed how she'd gathered intelligence at U.S. shipyards and how she'd used the code provided by Japanese Naval Attaché Ichiro Yokoyama to craft the letters. What we'll never know is why the letters had been, thankfully, incorrectly addressed.

Below: Dickinson's doll shop in New York City in 1937 and one of the five letters mailed by Dickinson and decoded by the FBI Lab.

January 27 1942

My Most Gracious Friend

Please forgive my delay in writing to thank you for your kindness in sending my family the beautiful Christmas gifts. The girls were especially pleased.

I have been so very busy these days,this is the first time I have been over to Seattle for weeks.I came over today to meet my son who is here from Portland on business and to get my little granddaughters doll repaired. I must tell you this amusing story,the wife of an important business associate gave her an old German bisque Doll dressed in a Hulu Grass skirt.It is a cheap horrid thing I do Not like it and wish we did not have to have it about.Well I broke this awful doll last month now the person who gave the doll is coming to visit us very soon.I walked all over Seattle to get someo[n]e to repair it,no one at home could or would try the task. Now I expect all the damages to be repaired by the first week in February.In the meanwhile I hope and pray the Important gentlemen's wife will not come to visit us intill after that date.

directly. In June 1942, for example, German subs dropped off four saboteurs each in Long Island and northeastern Florida. The Nazis had trained these men in explosives, chemistry, and secret writing. But one of the men—George Dasch—got cold feet and turned himself in to the FBI in New York City. Agents quickly tracked down and arrested the remaining seven saboteurs before any harm was done.

George Dasch

The Bureau's domestic counterintelligence work continued full force as well, with plenty of successes. The FBI employed a variety of double agents to disrupt enemy espionage, set up radio networks to gather intelligence and spread disinformation, and used its growing scientific capabilities to track down spies like Velvalee Dickinson (see page 37).

All of these new responsibilities required an influx of manpower—and Congress readily delivered the resources. The FBI's rolls swelled from just 2,400 agents and support employees in 1940 to a war-time peak of more than 13,000 in 1944. Because of its National Academy training regimen for law enforcement executives, the Bureau had a ready pool of experienced graduates that it could tap into for new special agents. The FBI also brought on board huge numbers of professionals for its fingerprinting, scientific, and

records management operations; its Identification Division grew so large that it had to be moved to a federal armory larger than a football field (see page 40).

The nation breathed a sigh of relief when the Axis powers finally collapsed. Germany—with most of its troops captured and Berlin surrounded by advancing American and Soviet forces—was the first to raise the white flag, in May 1945. After being soundly defeated in the field and experiencing the horror of two A-bombs, Japan surrendered in August.

June 1942
Nazi saboteurs land on U.S. soil but are quickly captured

August 1946
Atomic Energy Act makes FBI responsible for protecting the security of nuclear secrets

The Mysterious Russian Letter

In the summer of 1943, an anonymous typewritten letter in Russian suddenly appeared at FBI Headquarters.

Talk about intrigue: the disgruntled writer accused more than ten Soviet diplomats in the U.S. of being spies, including the Soviet Vice-Consuls in San Francisco and New York and the Second Secretary of the Soviet Embassy in Washington—Vasilli Zubilin. The author even claimed (falsely) that Zubilin was spying for the Nazis.

The charges were hard to believe. The Russians—our country's allies in World War II—spying on the U.S.?

At the time, the FBI had only just begun investigating the extent of Soviet operations in America, with most resources heavily dedicated to Axis espionage and sabotage cases.

Now, this letter. What to make of it? Parts of it were strange and unbelievable, like the Nazi connections, but other parts confirmed things the FBI already knew or suspected. It was clear that its author was credible and well versed in Soviet intelligence in the United States.

Four months earlier, in fact, agents had learned that Zubilin had spoken with—and slipped money to—a Communist Party official named Steve Nelson. Zubilin's aim? To infiltrate a Berkeley, California, lab doing work for the Manhattan Project, America's secret atomic bomb program. The FBI passed what it learned about Zubilin's spying to the War Department, which had primary investigative jurisdiction on the project. After the war ended, agents would investigate other, more serious attempts to steal U.S. A-bomb secrets, but that's another story (see page 48).

In the meantime, the Bureau had a predicate to take a closer look at Soviet espionage. Agents launched a major investigation to discover the potential interrelationships of Soviet diplomats, the Communist Party of the United States, and the Communist International party, or Comintern.

Through the case—called COMRAP, for "Comintern Apparatus"—the FBI learned that Soviet spying was a significant threat, which helped the Bureau prepare for the Cold War to come.

Photo of Vasilli Zubilin in 1943 and a copy of the mysterious letter that mentioned him

TOP SECRET

Mr. HOOVER,

Exceptional circumstances impel us to inform you of the activities of the so-called director of the Soviet Intelligence in this country. This "Soviet" intelligence officer genuinely occupies a very high post in the GPU (now NKVD), enjoys to a vast extent the confidence of the Soviet Government, but in fact, as we know very accurately, works for Japan himself, while his wife (works) for Germany. Thus, under cover of the name of the USSR, he is a dangerous enemy of the USSR and the U.S.A. The vast organisation of permanent staff [KADROVYE] workers of the NKVD under his command in the U.S.A. does not suspect that, thanks to the treachery of their director, they are also inflicting frightful harm on their own country. In this same false position is also their whole network of agents, among whom are many U.S. citizens, and finally BROWDER himself, who has immediate contact with them. BROWDER passes on to him very important information about the U.S.A., thinking that all this goes to MOSCOW, but, as you see, it all goes to the Japanese and Germans. ¶ The "Director of the Soviet Intelligence" here is ZUBILIN, Vasilij, 2nd secretary in the embassy of the USSR, his real name is ZARUBIN, V., deputy head of the Foreign Intelligence Directorate [UPRAVLENIE] of the NKVD. He personally deals with getting agents into and out of the U.S.A. illegally, organises secret radio-stations and manufactures forged documents. His closest assistants are:
1. His wife, directs political intelligence here, has a vast network of agents in almost all ministries including the State

The FBI's fingerprinting work grew
so massive during the war that it had
to be moved to a federal armory larger than a football field.

War was over. At least for the moment.

A more insidious, protracted conflict, it turns out, would soon be underway. The ambitious Soviets had snapped up several Eastern European countries as war prizes, and its "Iron Curtain" would soon descend, physically and symbolically dividing east and west, communism and democracy. The U.S. and Soviet Union—the two primary superpowers on the block—would spend the next four decades trying to gain the military and political upper hand. With both countries stockpiling nuclear weapons, the stakes were high.

The FBI's growing national security capabilities would be crucial in the coming Cold War, but it quickly realized that it had a lot of catching up to do with the U.S.S.R. Although the Bureau

had learned of Soviet espionage during World War II through its investigation of Russian diplomat and spy Vasili Zubilin (see page 39) and others, its war-time counterintelligence resources were overwhelmingly and understandably focused on the Axis threats. Our "allies" the Soviets, meanwhile, had used the war years to sneak agents into sensitive positions in our government. They had even subverted some of our nation's policies and sought to influence our intelligence practices.

The defections of Soviet code clerk Igor Guzenko in the late summer of 1945 and U.S. citizen turned Soviet spy Elizabeth Bentley a few weeks later led to the FBI's first major breaks in learning how much damage had been done to national security. In 1948, revelations on Soviet espionage triggered congressional hearings and front-page headlines when *Time* magazine editor

FBI agents on a stakeout during a kidnapping case

March 21, 1947
FBI ordered to investigate federal employee loyalty

March 14, 1950
"Ten Most Wanted Fugitives" program launched

The Spying Game

Below are some of the espionage tools and tricks uncovered in FBI investigations.

Tape recorder used to record coded instructions

This hollow cuff link stored secret messages

The "Dead Drop" is a place where intelligence operatives leave secrets, money, or instructions. The broken step (later repaired) shown here was used to pass spy messages in 1955.

This sanding block opened to disclose a sealed package, a one-time cipher pad containing 250 double pages of gold and silver foil

Carefully hollowed containers for transmitting microfilmed messages to Moscow

Whittaker Chambers accused a prominent New Deal attorney named Alger Hiss of spying for the Russians; challenged by Hiss to prove his claims, Chambers produced solid evidence that Hiss had passed him classified information for the Soviets.

**William Fisher
(aka Rudolf Abel)**

Alger Hiss

Ultimately, the tide began turning. Using strong detective work and cutting-edge intelligence collection and analysis tools, the FBI and its partners in the intelligence community—along with allies in Canada and Great Britain—began dismantling Soviet spy networks. An Army Signal Corps project—later code-named Venona—helped this effort a great deal, providing the FBI with intelligence-rich telegrams sent from Soviet spies back to Moscow. Over the course of the project, which ran from 1943 until 1980, the FBI and its partners identified some 350 persons connected with Soviet intelligence. Venona was so sensitive that it was kept under wraps for some four decades; its information was not even used in court cases to keep from tipping off the Russians. The Bureau quietly used Venona intelligence, for example, to uncover an espionage ring run by Julius and Ethel Rosenberg that passed secrets on the atomic bomb to the Soviet Union.

By the early 1950s, the FBI and its allies had largely purged the federal government of dangerous moles and moved to become more proactive in infiltrating and deceiving Soviet intelligence. These successes forced the Soviets to retool their espionage efforts and begin relying on "illegal" agents—professional spies using various covers to hide in society at large. A good example was William Fisher (aka Rudolf Abel), who posed as a retired photographer while secretly recruiting and supervising Soviet spies. The FBI captured him in 1957 (see page 49).

The Bureau's traditional criminal work, of course, continued during the early Cold War—from the Brinks robbery in 1950 (see page 47) to the kidnapping and murder of young Bobby Greenlease in 1953. The FBI also launched a key crime-fighting tool in March 1950—the "Ten Most Wanted Fugitives" list—which has since enlisted the help of a ubiquitous news media and a watchful public to capture more than 450 of the nation's most dangerous criminals.

As the FBI headed into the middle of the decade, though, a rising criminal challenge based on an age-old problem—racial prejudice—would soon dominate the national stage and require the Bureau's growing involvement.

March 1951
"Trial of the Century" leads to conviction of Rosenbergs

The Black Dahlia

On the morning of January 15, 1947, a mother taking her child for a walk in a Los Angeles neighborhood stumbled upon a gruesome sight: the body of a young naked woman sliced clean in half at the waist.

The body was just a few feet from the sidewalk and posed in such a way that the mother reportedly thought it was a mannequin at first glance. Despite the extensive mutilation and cuts on the body, there wasn't a drop of blood at the scene, indicating that the young woman had been killed elsewhere.

The ensuing investigation was led by the L.A. Police Department. The FBI was asked to help, and it quickly identified the body—just 56 minutes, in fact, after getting blurred fingerprints via "Soundphoto" (a primitive fax machine used by news services) from Los Angeles.

The young woman turned out to be a 22-year-old Hollywood hopeful named Elizabeth Short—later dubbed the "Black Dahlia" by the press for her rumored penchant for sheer black clothes and for the *Blue Dahlia* movie out at that time.

Short's prints actually appeared twice in the FBI's massive collection (more than 100 million were on file at the time)—first, because she had applied for a job as a clerk at the commissary of the Army's Camp Cooke in California in January 1943; second, because she had been arrested by the Santa Barbara police for underage drinking seven months later. The Bureau also had her "mug shot" in its files and provided it to the press.

In support of L.A. police, the FBI ran records checks on potential suspects and conducted interviews across the nation. Based on early suspicions that the murderer may have had skills in dissection because the body was so cleanly cut, agents were also asked to check out a group of students at the University of Southern California Medical School. And, in a tantalizing potential break in the case, the Bureau searched for a match to fingerprints found on an anonymous letter that may have been sent to authorities by the killer, but the prints weren't in FBI files.

Who killed the Black Dahlia and why? It's a mystery. The murderer has never been found, and given how much time has passed, probably never will be. The legend grows…

**An L.A. Police
Department flyer
on Elizabeth Short**

SPECIAL
Daily Police Bulletin
For Circulation Among Police Officers Exclusively

Issued Daily Except Saturday Sunday & Holidays by Police Printing Bureau

OFFICIAL PUBLICATION OF POLICE DEPARTMENT, CITY OF LOS ANGELES, CALIFORNIA

CHIEF'S OFFICE, City Hall (Phone MIchigan 5211—Connecting all Stations and Depts.) C. B. HORRALL, Chief of Police

Vol. 40   Tuesday, January 21, 1947   No. 1

WANTED INFORMATION ON ELIZABETH SHORT
Between Dates January 9 and 15, 1947

Description: Female, American, 22 years, 5 ft. 6 in., 118 lbs., black hair, green eyes, very attractive, bad teeth, finger nails chewed to quick. This subject found brutally murdered, body severed and mutilated January 15, 1947, at 39th and Norton.

Subject on whom information wanted last seen January 9, 1947 when she got out of car at Biltmore wearing black suit, no collar on coat, probably Cardigan style, white fluffy blouse, full-length beige coat, carried black plastic h…

FAMOUS CASES

The Duquesne Spy Ring

How's this for being a step ahead of the enemy? Before America ever fired a shot in World War II, the FBI had rolled up a massive ring of Nazi spies operating on U.S. soil—33 in all, ranging from Paul Bante to Bertram Wolfgang Zenzinger. By December 13, 1941—just six days after Pearl Harbor—every member of the group had either pled guilty or been convicted at trial, including its ringleader Fritz Duquesne.

It all began when a lone German-American refused to give in to Nazi aggression and hatred. His name was William Sebold, and he served the Allied cause by becoming a double agent for the FBI.

Fritz Duquesne

Sebold was a naturalized U.S. citizen who worked in industrial and aircraft plants throughout the U.S. and South America after leaving his native land in 1921. During a return trip to Germany in 1939, Sebold was "persuaded" by high-ranking members of the German Secret Service to spy on America. Sebold received espionage training in Hamburg (including how to work a short-wave radio), but not before secretly visiting the American consulate in Cologne and telling officials there that he wanted to cooperate with the FBI.

The Bureau was waiting when Sebold returned to New York City in February 1940. He'd been instructed by the Nazis to take on the persona of "Harry Sawyer," a diesel engineer consultant. He was then to meet with various spies, pass along instructions to them from Germany, receive messages in return, and transmit them back in code to Germany.

With Sebold's masterful acting, the FBI played right along with the ruse, using some deceits of its own.

First, FBI Lab engineers built a secret shortwave radio transmitting station on Long Island. There, FBI agents pretending to be Sebold sent authentic-sounding messages to his German superiors for some 16 straight months. Over that time more than 300 messages were sent and another 200 were received from the Nazis.

Top right: Agents secretly filmed the many spies who passed through Sebold's bogus office. Bottom right: Sebold talks with Duquesne, who was unaware that FBI agents were taping the whole episode behind a two-way mirror

Second, FBI agents helped set up an office for "Harry" in Manhattan where he could receive visiting spies. The office was outfitted with hidden microphones and a two-way mirror where agents could watch and film everything going on. With cameras secretly rolling, Sebold met with a string of Nazis who wished to pass secret and sensitive national defense and wartime information to the Gestapo.

One of those visitors was Duquesne, a veteran spy who served

as the group's leader. In Sebold's rigged office, Duquesne explained how fires could be started at industrial plants and shared photographs and plans he'd stolen from a plant in Delaware describing a new bomb being made in the U.S.

Another one of the spies, agents learned, was preparing a bomb of his own and even delivered dynamite and detonation caps to Sebold.

Once the Bureau had enough information to pinpoint the members of the ring and enough evidence for an airtight case, the 33 spies were arrested. Nineteen quickly pled guilty; the rest were found guilty at trial in the days following the Pearl Harbor attack.

As a result of the massive investigation, the FBI—and America—entered the war with confidence that there was no major German espionage network hidden in U.S. society.

FAMOUS CASES

ND-98: The Long Island Double Agent

The unmistakable clatter of a telegraph key sounded in a small room of a secluded house on Long Island. A coded message was being hammered out by an agent code-named ND-98. On the other side of the Atlantic, a member of the Abwehr, the Nazi government's most important intelligence service, was poised to receive the message.

It was February 1942, and it was ND-98's first radio message to his German bosses. He wasn't sure if his message would be acknowledged, nor if he would be accepted as an Abwehr spy and his future revelations passed on to key members of the government for information and action.

Several others also waited in that small Long Island room, hoping that ND-98 would be successful. They nervously fingered their FBI badges. In fact, "ND-98" was not the Abwehr's codename for this particular spy; it was the Bureau's. In real life, this man was the owner of an import-export business who had offered his services to the FBI as a double agent...for money. It was an opportunity not to be missed.

ND-98 was not the first double agent recruited by the FBI. Beginning in early 1940, the FBI had identified German agents in America, "turned" them, and successfully used their identities without tipping their masters. In short order, the Bureau had made good progress in learning the modus operandi of the German intelligence services, the identities of their agents, and ways to counter their operations. It was also able to send false information to the Nazi government, much like the wider and highly successful British network of double agent operations against Hitler's forces throughout the war.

Back in Long Island, ND-98 finished the transmission and leaned back in his chair. The tension in the room crackled. Then, suddenly, the Nazi reply came back loud and clear. Tell us about troop movements, it said, and about arms and aircraft production. The Bureau, in turn, was happy to comply. Through ND-98 and his telegraph key, lots of information was sent—all carefully prepared to convince the Nazis it was genuine without divulging anything of real value.

And from time to time, the FBI would insert false information (carefully cleared with the Army and Navy) that would misdirect the Nazi government and aid the Allied cause. This was the icing on the cake. In key situations, ND-98's radio was able to suggest that the U.S. was going to attack in one place on a certain date. German military leaders would amass their defenses there accordingly, when in reality, Allied armed forces were attacking

another location, less well defended because of the false intelligence. ND-98 was able to help in some Allied battlefield successes through the D-Day invasion at Normandy.

ND-98's long string of broadcasts and his role in providing disinformation at key phases of the war made this double agent one of the Bureau's most successful intelligence operations during World War II.

Top: Radio station equipment in Clinton, Maryland in 1941
Bottom: Working model of a portable two-way radio developed in 1947

FAMOUS CASES

The Case of the Ragtime Bug

Here's a hypothetical: what would you do?

It's February 1944 in New York City—wartime. One of your informants contacts you and tells you that the leadership of the Communist Party of the United States is planning a secret meeting in a midtown Manhattan recording studio.

Here's what you know as background: This organization has accepted secret money and foreign control from the Soviet Union since its formation. It has conspired to commit passport fraud; to provide cover for foreign agents; to collect and pass U.S. secrets to Soviet Intelligence; and to recruit spies. And that you are on firm legal ground to find out the purpose of the meeting. You have heard that its leaders—William Z. Foster and Earl Browder—are wrangling over the future direction the organization should take: to support or not support the U.S. war effort.

U.S. Communist Party leader Earl Browder (center) at his final campaign rally for U.S. President in November 1936. Browder won only 80,000 votes in the presidential election and was expelled from the party in 1946 after he drifted away from hardline communist ideology.

Do you: 1) Install a hidden Closed Circuit TV camera in the meeting room studio? 2) Hide under a sofa in the room? 3) Round up all your musically talented employees and put them in rehearsal there?

If you guessed #1, you get partial credit, though CCTV surveillance hadn't been invented yet. If you guessed option #3, you were entirely correct.

A call went out to every FBI employee in the New York City area: Report in if you can play a musical instrument, it said.

First, ahead of time, the Bureau rented the studio where the Community Party of the U.S. was to meet. While some agents struck up a little ragtime there, others placed listening devices throughout the room.

Next, the Bureau rented the studio next door and "played" there throughout the long meeting—one set of "musicians" arriving with their instruments, playing some compositions, then departing and letting in the next "combo" to play new music, all to

keep up the ruse while a handful of agents manned the bugs.

"I think Comrade Browder [the Communist Party leader in the U.S. at that time] is also subject to making a mistake," Foster was heard to say. Browder, he argued, was wrong in wanting to support the U.S. in the war—the party should not forget the class struggle, and it must not support the capitalists.

Ironically, Comrade Foster was right, by Soviet lights, but not at that particular moment in time. Moscow briefly forsook the party line to support Browder's idea because it needed the help of its U.S. military ally in the wartime effort. Foster lost much prestige and had to acquiesce, for the time, to Browder's leadership.

Less than a year-and-a-half later, though, Moscow's tactics again shifted. A major European communist denounced Browder, a signal taken by all to be at Moscow's command. He was immediately expelled from the Communist Party of the U.S. and his nemesis, William Foster, took over. It was back to business as usual.

FAMOUS CASES

The Great Brinks Robbery

It was billed as "the perfect crime." And it nearly was.

On January 17, 1950, employees of the security firm Brinks, Inc., in Boston, were closing for the day, returning sacks of undelivered cash, checks, and other material to the company safe on the second floor.

Shortly before 7:30 p.m., they were surprised by five men—heavily disguised, quiet as mice, wearing gloves to avoid leaving fingerprints and soft shoes to muffle noise. The thieves quickly bound the employees and began hauling away the loot. Within minutes, they'd stolen more than $1.2 million in cash and another $1.5 million in checks and other securities, making it the largest robbery in the U.S. at the time.

The evidence left behind? Paltry. Just some tape and rope used to gag and bind the Brink's employees.

Anthony Pino

Disguise used

Boston police and Bureau agents got to work within minutes of the bank's call—scouring the crime scene, identifying missing items, questioning the employees (and checking for clues and signs of collusion), and blanketing the wider community of criminals and their supporters.

Slowly key clues began to emerge. In February, a police officer found a gun stolen during the heist. The next month, FBI agents located the getaway truck that was used—at least part of it, as the criminals had cut it to pieces and dumped it at a scrap yard.

Also taking shape was a group of key suspects: Anthony Pino, a local hoodlum whose M.O. fit the crime; Joe McGinnis, a Boston underworld figure who'd been with Pino that night; and Joseph O'Keefe and Staley Gusciora, both local ex-cons who knew Pino, had a reputation for being able to handle guns (the "strong arms" needed for such a heist), had weak alibis, and had family near where the getaway truck was recovered.

They might have gotten away with it, but the criminals had all agreed to sit on the money for a few years and slowly launder it to avoid detection. And with so much free time on their hands, they got into trouble. O'Keefe and Gusciora landed in jail for

various crimes. The others also had problems keeping low.

Eventually, the oft-imprisoned O'Keefe grew bitter and began complaining that he didn't get his fair share of the money. After several unsuccessful attempts on his life by his confederates, he decided to tell the full story of the 11-man job to FBI agents.

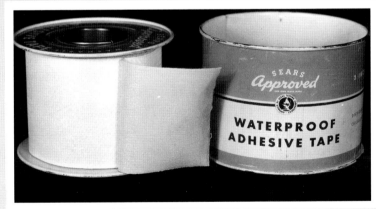

Top: Burlap bags with pieces of the truck used in the robbery found in a local junkyard
Bottom: Waterproof tape left at the scene of the crime

In the end, the painstaking work of the Bureau, the Boston police, and others led to the arrest of six gang members in January 1956. Two others were already in prison, one was dead, and two were placed on the Ten Most Wanted Fugitives list and later caught. More than half of the money was soon recovered, and the suspects went to trial. On October 5, 1956, a Boston jury found each of them guilty.

The "perfect crime" had a perfect ending—for everyone but the robbers.

FAMOUS CASES

Atom Bomb Spies

It was a somber statement that stunned the nation.

"We have evidence that within recent weeks an atomic explosion occurred in the U.S.S.R.," President Truman told America on September 23, 1949. The Soviets had their first nuclear weapon, and suddenly, the Cold War grew a lot warmer.

Meanwhile, the FBI had already been gathering evidence on who helped the Soviets unlock the secrets of the atom bomb by stealing our nation's secrets on how to build it.

Klaus Fuchs

Thanks to intelligence from a brilliant Army cryptographic breakthrough now known as the Venona Project (see page 43), the Bureau had learned just days before Truman's announcement that such a theft had indeed taken place. FBI agents rushed to Los Alamos, New Mexico and other key sites for atomic plants in the U.S. and began extensive interviews and research. The Bureau also mined its many intelligence sources.

Harry Gold

The resulting clues and intelligence pointed to Klaus Fuchs, a British physicist and secret communist who'd been sent to work on the Manhattan Project at Los Alamos National Laboratory. Klaus had since returned to England, so the Bureau contacted MI5 (British counterintelligence), which began keeping an eye on him. On February 2, 1950, Fuchs was arrested by the British and confessed to giving a trove of nuclear secrets to the Soviets over the course of eight years.

Fuchs said that he passed his materials through a stocky American chemist whom he knew only as "Raymond." Through painstaking investigative work, the FBI tracked down that man as well. His name was Harry Gold, and he, too, confessed to being part of the espionage ring.

Evidence of the conspiracy continued to widen. Gold began talking, leading agents to David Greenglass, an American who worked at the Los Alamos lab. Greenglass also admitted his involvement in passing atomic secrets. And he told agents that the leader of the spy ring he worked for was Julius Rosenberg, who was married to his sister Ethel. Both were strident communists.

Julius Rosenberg, agents learned, had been running a ring devoted to stealing military technology and had taken very important information about U.S. radar, missile guidance systems, and

As the jury deliberates during their trial, Julius and Ethel Rosenberg ride with Morton Sobell (far left), another convicted member of Rosenberg's spy ring

atomic energy research. Greenglass said he had given Rosenberg a variety of classified documents, including sketches of a Nagasaki-like atomic bomb and handwritten reports on work going on at Los Alamos.

This investigative legwork was backed up once again by Venona—what one historian has called the "Holy Grail" of Cold War counterintelligence. For example, one 1944 telegram intercepted from the Soviets read in part: "Information on LIBERAL's wife. Surname that of her husband, first name Ethel, 29 years old. Married five years…A FELLOWCOUNTRYMAN." Agents determined that LIBERAL referred to Julius Rosenberg; "fellow countryman" was code for a communist party member. Other telegrams suggested that Ethel knew about her husband's work.

Venona intelligence was invaluable, clearly identifying Rosenberg as a Soviet agent and confirming statements made by Gold and Greenglass. But it couldn't be used in court, since it would have exposed the secret project and revealed American counterespionage practices. In the end, though, both Julius and Ethel Rosenberg were arrested, convicted, and ultimately executed for their crimes.

FAMOUS CASES
Hollow Nickel, Hidden Agent

What's a nickel worth?

No, it's not a riddle. It's a case straight from the pages of FBI history.

It all started in June 1953, when a Brooklyn newspaper boy picked up a nickel he'd just dropped. Almost like magic, the coin split in half. And inside was a tiny photograph, showing a series of numbers too small to read.

Even if the boy kept up with the front page news on the papers he delivered, he probably never would have guessed that this extraordinary coin was the product of one of the most vital national security issues of the day: the growing Cold War between the world's two nuclear powers, the U.S. and the Soviet Union.

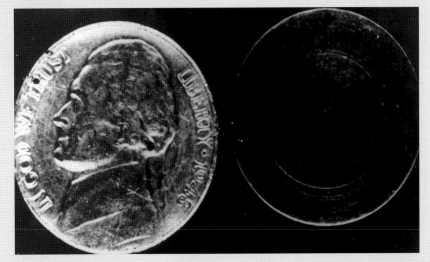

The coin ultimately made its way to the FBI, which opened a counterintelligence case, knowing the coin suggested there was an active spy in New York City. But who?

Reino Hayhanen

New York agents quickly began working to trace the hollow nickel. They talked to the ladies who passed the nickel on to the delivery boy, with no success. They talked to local novelty store owners, but none had seen anything like it. A lot of shoe leather was ruined, but no hot leads emerged.

Meanwhile, the coin itself underwent expert examination. FBI Lab scientists in Washington pored over it. They immediately realized the photograph contained a coded message, but they couldn't crack it. The coin did yield clues, however. The typeprint, Lab experts concluded, must have come from a foreign typewriter. Metallurgy showed that the back half was from a coin minted during World War II. Ultimately, the coin was filed away, but not forgotten.

The key break came four years later, when a Russian spy named Reino Hayhanen defected to the United States. Hayhanen—really the American born Eugene Maki—shared all kinds of secrets on Soviet spies. He led FBI agents to one out-of-the-way hiding place, called a "dead drop," where FBI agents found a hollowed-out bolt with a typewritten message inside. When asked about it, Hayhanen said the Soviets had given him all kinds of hollowed-out objects: pens, screws, batteries, even coins. He turned over one such coin, which instantly reminded agents of the Brooklyn

nickel. The link was made.

From there, Hayhanen put investigators on the trail of his case officer, a Soviet spy named "Mark" who was operating without diplomatic cover and under several false identities.

After painstaking detective work, agents figured out that "Mark" was really William Fisher, aka Rudolf Abel, who was arrested on June 21, 1957. Though Abel refused to talk, his hotel room and office revealed an important prize: a treasure trove of modern espionage equipment.

Abel was eventually convicted of espionage and sentenced to a long jail term. In 1962, he was exchanged for American U-2 pilot Francis Gary Powers, who had been shot down over the U.S.S.R. and held prisoner there.

In the end, a nickel was worth a great deal: the capture of a Soviet spy and the protection of a nation.

**Top: The actual hollow nickel
Bottom: The coded message found inside**

And Justice for All, 1954-1971

When nine black-robed Supreme Court judges sat down behind their mahogany bench on spring day in 1954 and declared that a separate system of schools for blacks and whites was not really equal after all, turning Jim Crow on its ear, the winds of change began to blow across America.

They'd blow harder still when a 42-year-old black woman named Rosa Parks, after a long day at work, refused to give up her bus seat to a white man on the first day of December in 1955,

and when a young, then unknown Baptist preacher named Martin Luther King, Jr., took up her cause and led a successful bus boycott in Montgomery, Alabama.

"We shall overcome," blacks and whites alike soon began singing, and what they hoped to overcome was the deep-seated prejudice and injustice that existed towards African-Americans in this country for far too long. Thomas Jefferson had penned the classic phrase, "All men are created equal," nearly two centuries earlier, calling it a self-evident truth. But the question was, did we as a nation really mean it? Could we deliver justice for all? The civil rights movement aimed to find out.

Wrapped up in this struggle in the ensuing years would be the FBI. It had cut its investigative teeth on civil rights crimes; a dozen of the first 34 special agents were experts in "peonage"—the modern-day equivalent of slave labor. The Bureau had begun battling the KKK in the 1920s (see page 15), and for years it had handled so-called "color of law" cases involving brutality or other civil rights crimes by state and local authorities.

Rosa Parks with Martin Luther King, Jr. in 1955 In 1947, for instance, after a local sheriff and his deputy stood by and watched a mob dressed in Klan robes burn crosses and beat a handful of blacks in Georgia, the FBI's investigation led

December 14, 1957
Mafia meeting exposed in Apalachin, New York

to the conviction of both officers. The federal grand jury singled out the work of the special agents in the case, resolving that "…by their great fidelity and singleness of purpose in developing the information in the Dade County, Georgia, conspiracy trial [they] have gone far beyond the line of duty to aid, assist and protect the citizens of the United States and to further the cause of equity and justice in America."

Still, the FBI had its jurisdictional limits. Lynching in those days was not a federal crime, nor were bias-based attacks and most murders (to this day, hate crime is not a specific federal offense). States guarded their rights jealously, and local authorities often loudly complained if the FBI interfered in race-related crimes in their communities. Even when the Bureau did have jurisdiction in civil rights-related cases, that didn't guarantee the cooperation of witnesses. And in the Deep South especially, white-dominated juries all too often disregarded the facts and evidence Bureau agents and others put together, letting the guilty go scot-free in remarkable miscarriages of justice.

Above: A Freedom Riders bus is set on fire in Alabama, on May 14, 1961
Left: A KKK cross burning

June 12, 1963
Medgar Evers murdered in Mississippi

Around the FBI

A few scenes in the FBI during the time period. Left top: The FBI's massive crime indexing files. Left bottom: Cincinnati agents strike an informal pose in 1949. Right: Use of teletype machines in the 1950s.

A good example of the FBI's limitations—and the prevailing state of justice below the Mason-Dixon line—came in August 1955, when a visiting black teenager from Chicago named Emmett Till reportedly whistled at a white woman in a Mississippi country store. Till was kidnapped, beaten beyond recognition, shot in the head, and thrown into the Tallahatchie River with a large fan tied to his neck. The woman's husband and his half-brother were accused of murder, but an all-white jury acquitted them both. The FBI was prevented from investigating by the Department of Justice, which ruled that no federal laws had been broken despite the horrific nature of the crime. In 2004, when times (and laws) were different, Bureau and Mississippi officials reopened the case, but with the main culprits long since dead and credible evidence against others hard to come by, no charges were filed.

As the 1950s turned into the early 1960s, the backlash against blacks by the Klan and like-minded racists became increasingly violent as the civil rights movement gained momentum. In 1961, angry white mobs repeatedly attacked busloads of "freedom riders" who traveled to the South to help integrate public facilities.

The next year, violence and riots erupted when James Meredith became the first black student to enroll at the University of Mis-

November 22, 1963
President Kennedy assassinated in Dallas

Joe's Barbeque Cooks the Mob

On a mid-November day in 1957, a soft drink bottler named Joseph Barbara hosted a get-together at his rural estate in Apalachin, a small town just west of Binghamton, New York. He called it a soft drink convention. It was anything but.

Sergeant Edgar Croswell of the New York State Police was intensely interested in the gathering. He'd observed suspected criminals at the house before and was suspicious. With smoke rising from Barbara's outdoor grill, Croswell and Trooper Vincent Vasisko began to take down the license plate numbers of the luxury cars jammed in the driveway.

Suddenly Barbara's guests noticed…and panicked. Some fled to the woods; others dashed for their cars. Sergeant Croswell ordered an immediate roadblock and soon had detained 62 guests in order to check their identification. Among them were Joseph Bonanano, Russell Bufalino, Carlo Gambino, Vito Genovese, Antonio Magaddino, Joseph Proface, John Scalish, and Santos Traficante—a veritable Who's Who of what is now called the "Mob," the "Mafia," or "La Cosa Nostra."

Croswell's important detective work exploded nationally. The FBI, for its part, immediately checked the names taken by the officers. It had information in its files on 53 of the mobsters; 40 had criminal records. Croswell's discovery led the FBI to intensify its interest in these figures (not begin it, as some have speculated) and to arrest mobsters who violated federal law. In part because of events at Apalachin, the FBI realized that local and regional crime lords were conspiring and began to adjust its strategy accordingly.

That strategy had taken shape four years earlier, when the New York office—facing rising mobster activity—had specifically asked to open intelligence files on 30 top hoodlums in the city to get a general picture of their activities and to keep an eye out for violations of federal law. On August 25, 1953, the FBI launched a national "Top Hoodlum Program," asking all field offices to gather information on mobsters in their territories and to report it regularly to Washington to build a centralized collection of intelligence on racketeers.

It's important to understand: at the time, most racketeering activities—including gambling and loan sharking—were beyond the Bureau's jurisdictional reach. Still, the FBI needed to build a bank of information to better understand the threat and to be prepared if federal laws were broken.

With the extra exposure provided at Apalachin, this program ultimately produced a wealth of information about organized crime activities. And in 1963, thanks in part to the FBI, the

first major Mafia turncoat—Joseph Valachi—publicly spilled the beans before a Senate subcommittee, naming names and exposing plenty of secrets about organized crime history, operations, and rituals.

But the Bureau still needed legislative tools to get past the small time crooks and connect them with those barons of the underworld. Congress powerfully delivered, with illegal gambling laws that unlocked Mafia financial networks and with laws like the Omnibus Crime Control Act of 1968 and the Racketeer Influenced and Corrupt Organizations Act of 1970. All of this helped the FBI's campaign against the mob turn a corner, setting the stage for some important victories in the coming years.

**Top: Joseph Valachi testifies before the Senate on October 1, 1963, showing how he was initiated into the Mafia by having to burn a crumbled ball of paper in his hands while taking the mob oath.
Bottom: Barbara's home in New York, site of the mob meeting**

Neshoba County Sheriff Lawrence Rainey, flanked by FBI agents, is brought to court in October 1964 in connection with the Mississippi Burning murders

sissippi. In May 1963, Birmingham police commissioner "Bull" Connor—a known KKK member—unleashed police dogs and fire hoses on peaceful protestors. The following month, a leading black civil rights activist named Medgar Evers was shot dead in the driveway of his Mississippi home. Three months later, four young black girls were killed when a powerful bomb exploded in the basement of the Sixteenth Street Baptist Church in Birmingham (see page 60). The FBI investigated the Evers murder and the Birmingham bombing, but it had no jurisdiction in the case of Connor's actions.

A turning point came in 1964 at the start of "Freedom Summer," a massive campaign to register blacks to vote in Mississippi. Three young civil rights activists—two white, one black—were brutally murdered by the KKK there, with the full cooperation of local law enforcement. The FBI quickly identified the culprits in a case that came to be called "Mississippi Burning" (see page 61), arresting 21 men in Mississippi by early December. Martin Luther King responded to the news by saying, "I must commend the Federal Bureau of Investigation for the work they have done

in uncovering the perpetrators of this dastardly act. It renews again my faith in democracy."

He spoke a little too soon, as justice in the courtroom was a different matter. Most of the men went free or were convicted of lesser charges; it took until 2005 before Edgar Ray Killen, one of the chief conspirators, was convicted of manslaughter. Still, the outrage at the killings helped spur passage of the Civil Rights Act of 1964 less a month later and the Voting Rights Act of 1965 the following summer.

The 1964 law in particular—which banned segregation on a wide scale, including in schools, public places, government, and the workplace—made a number of civil rights violations federal crimes for the first time and gave the Bureau the federal lead in combatting them. Today, protecting civil rights is one of the Bureau's top priorities, and, using its full suite of investigative and intelligence capabilities, it works closely with state and local authorities (in ways not possible decades ago) to prevent and address hate crime, human trafficking, police brutality, and other

June 21, 1964
Civil rights workers killed in "Mississippi Burning" case

September 1965
The FBI television show premiers starring Efrem Zimbalist, Jr.

Escape from Alcatraz

In its heyday, it was the ultimate maximum-security prison.

Located on a lonely island in the middle of San Francisco Bay, Alcatraz—aka "The Rock"—had held captives since the Civil War. But it was in 1934, the highpoint of the nation's war on crime and gangsters, that Alcatraz was re-fortified into the world's most secure prison. Its eventual inmates included dangerous public enemies like Al Capone, criminals who had a history of escapes, and the occasional odd character like the infamous "Birdman of Alcatraz."

Left: Alcatraz today
Below top: The fake head that fooled the guards
Below bottom: The hole made by the convicts to escape their cell

John Anglin

In the 1930s, Alcatraz was already a forbidding place, surrounded by the cold, rough waters of the Pacific. The redesign included tougher iron bars, a series of strategically positioned guard towers, and strict rules, including a dozen checks a day of the prisoners. Escape seemed near impossible.

Despite the odds, from 1934 until the prison was closed in 1963, 36 men tried 14 separate escapes. Nearly all were caught or didn't survive the attempt.

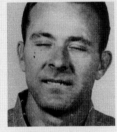

Clarence Anglin

The fate of three particular inmates, however, remains a mystery to this day.

On June 12, 1962, the early morning bed check turned up three missing convicts: John Anglin, his brother Clarence, and Frank Morris. In their beds were cleverly built dummy heads made of plaster, flesh-tone paint, and real human hair that apparently fooled the night guards. An intensive search began.

Frank Morris

The FBI was immediately asked to help. It set leads for offices nationwide to check for any records on the missing prisoners, interviewed relatives of the men, and asked boat operators in the Bay to watch for debris. Within two days, a packet of letters sealed in rubber and linked to the men was recovered. Later, some paddle-like pieces of wood and bits of rubber inner tube were found. A homemade life vest was also discovered washed up on Cronkhite Beach.

The FBI, the Coast Guard, Bureau of Prison authorities, and others began to find more evidence and piece together the ingenious escape plan, aided by a fourth plotter who didn't make it out of his cell in time and began providing information.

Investigators learned that the three escapees had carefully planned their escape. They used crude tools—including a homemade drill made from the motor of a broken vacuum cleaner—to loosen the air vents at the back of their cells. Once through, they made their way down an unguarded common corridor and climbed to the top of their cellblock inside the building, where they set up a secret workshop. There, they used a variety of stolen and donated materials to build what they needed to escape, including makeshift life preservers and a 6x14 foot rubber raft made out of more than 50 stolen raincoats.

On the evening of June 11, the Anglin brothers and Morris got into the corridor, climbed up and out through the ventilator, went to the prison roof, and gathered their gear stored there. Then, they shimmied down the bakery smoke stack at the rear of the cell house, climbed over the fence, snuck to the northeast shore of the island and launched their raft.

What happened next remains a mystery. Did they make it across the Bay, get to Angel Island, and then cross Raccoon Strait into Marin County as planned? Or did the wind and waves get the better of them?

The FBI officially closed its case on December 31, 1979, and turned over responsibility to the U.S. Marshals Service, which continues to investigate in the unlikely event the trio is still alive.

Right: In 1961, a special agent in the FBI Lab compares markings on wood chips found at a crime scene with the markings on an ax

crimes that take away the freedoms of the American people.

The civil rights movement ultimately began to unleash pent-up racial frustrations across the nation. Not all protests during the '60s were peaceful, as vocal groups like the Black Panthers that advocated armed resistance and police brutality (both real and perceived) began touching off more hostile confrontations, including a decade-long string of violent riots in Los Angeles, Detroit, and many other cities. In the first nine months of 1967 alone, more than 100 people were killed in rioting in more than 60 cities.

At the same time, opposition to the Vietnam War was growing, largely on college campuses but also among vocal leaders, including Reverend King. The conflict united many anti-establishment groups with a common goal, and non-violent protests calling for an end to the war were held nationwide. A new counterculture movement started taking shape, linked to and often led by folk and rock music and other forms of artistic expression. It was a time of high idealism, with many Americans advocating peace, freedom, individual rights, and a more open and tolerant society.

The movement, however, had a dark underbelly—namely, drugs, more radical protests (like the student takeover of Columbia University in New York in 1968), and violent attacks by some fringe groups. In 1970 alone, an estimated 3,000 bombings and 50,000 bomb threats took place across America. Violent left-wing radicals like the Weather Underground (see page 75) bombed a series of government buildings, including the U.S. Capitol and the Pentagon, in the '60s and early '70s.

Director Hoover meets with President John F. Kennedy and Attorney General Robert Kennedy in February 1961

On August 24, 1970, two students at the University of Wisconsin—where antiwar sentiments ran high—joined two other men in using a powerful homemade bomb to blow up Sterling Hall, which housed the Army Mathematics Research Center. One graduate student was killed and three others injured. The FBI quickly located three of the bombers; the fourth remains wanted to this day.

During this time the FBI was playing a key role through its criminal and national security cases. It took the lead in investigating the high-profile assassinations of national leaders like President Kennedy, Martin Luther King, and Senator Robert Kennedy (see page 62). It also investigated the Kent State shootings and other related incidents and attacks.

In this period no specific guidelines for FBI agents covering national security investigations had been developed by either Congress or the Justice Department (and none would be until 1976). The FBI therefore addressed domestic terrorism threats from militant left-wing groups as it had from communists in the 1950s and the KKK in the 1960s—using traditional investigative and intelligence techniques.

January 27, 1967
National Crime Information Center becomes operational

April 4, 1968
Dr. Martin Luther King, Jr., assassinated in Memphis

One such operation was "Cointelpro," short for Counterintelligence Program. Approved by the National Security Council in 1956, Cointelpro initially focused on disrupting the activities of the Community Party of the United States. Five years later it was expanded to include the Socialist Workers Party. The KKK was added in 1964, the Black Panther Party in 1967, and other leftist groups in ensuing years.

The goal of the operation was to get a better handle on domestic threats facing the nation and to prevent attacks by these organizations and their members. But some Cointelpro tactics went too far for the American people, who began to learn about the classified program after an FBI office in Media, Pennsylvania, was burglarized in 1971 by radicals and information was leaked to the press and Congress. In some cases, FBI agents had infiltrated groups, sowed discord among their members, and attempted to discredit their efforts—even when there was little or no evidence of unlawful activities. Hoover formally ended all Cointelpro operations in April 1971.

Though fairly limited in scope (about two-tenths of one percent of the FBI's investigative workload over a 15-year period), Cointelpro was later rightfully criticized by Congress and the country for abridging first amendment rights and for other reasons. The upshot—as you'll see in the next chapter—was stronger and much needed guidelines and controls over FBI national security investigations through a series of Attorneys' General orders and congressional legislation. But the ensuing new processes and regulations also made intelligence gathering more difficult for the FBI going forward, ultimately creating an artificial wall between criminal cases and national security investigations.

Despite missteps with Cointelpro, the FBI had not turned into a secret police force as some feared. The Bureau continued to be accountable to Congress and to the American people. And in the end, it had played an important and sometimes overlooked role in helping to ensure civil rights and domestic tranquility during a turbulent time for the nation through its criminal investigations and intelligence work.

In May 1972, a long chapter in FBI history came to a close with the passing of J. Edgar Hoover, who had served as Director for nearly a half century. In the years to come, he would often be remembered more for his failings than his strengths, but it was Hoover who had turned the Bureau into an investigative powerhouse, helped pioneer the application of scientific methods to fighting crime and terrorism, and greatly advanced the cause of law enforcement professionalism nationwide.

Over the next two decades, a series of Directors would focus on modernizing and reforming the Bureau as it confronted a growing palette of threats. It started with one of the most shocking, high-profile crimes in history.

On January 27, 1967, the FBI launched the National Crime Information Center, or NCIC, an electronic clearinghouse of criminal justice information (mug shots, crime records, etc.) that can be tapped into by police officers in squad cars or by police agencies nationwide.

October 15, 1970
Congress passes Organized Crime Control Act of 1970, which includes Racketeer Influenced and Corrupt Organization (RICO) law

FAMOUS CASES

The Case of the Mysterious Mid-Air Explosion

When a plane crashes at high speeds or explodes thousands of feet above the earth and evidence is blown to bits and scattered across miles of land or sea, how does the FBI help figure out whether or not it was foul play and who might be responsible?

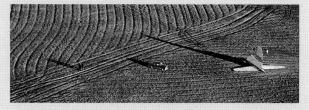

Jack Graham

The short answer: very painstakingly—by calling on a range of investigative and forensic capabilities and working closely with airline safety experts and other partners.

A good example—and an historic one, as it was the Bureau's first investigation of a major criminal attack on a U.S. airline—came in 1955.

On November 1, United Airlines Flight 629 crashed on a sugar beet farm some 35 miles north of its take-off from Denver. All 44 passengers and crew—including the wife of an aide to President Eisenhower and a young boy—were killed instantly.

Within days, FBI agents had a suspect—23-year-old Jack Graham, a disturbed delinquent who had packed a dynamite bomb in his mother's suitcase, driven her to the airport, kissed her goodbye, and taken out four insurance policies on her life.

Here's a quick run-down of how the case was solved:

First things first: the FBI Disaster Squad, a team of forensic

experts, traveled to the scene to help identify the bodies. Using civil fingerprint records, the investigators identified nearly half of the victims.

Meanwhile, an agent from the FBI Lab joined experts from the Civil Aeronautics Board and the airline and aircraft companies in examining the wreckage for clues. They methodically combed the crash area along the flight line, picking up pieces of the wreckage and marking their locations in a carefully plotted grid. Then, they placed the parts in a scaled-down grid at a Denver warehouse and reassembled the fuselage. Though the shell of the plane was basically intact, the right side of the plane had a jagged hole near the tail. The location? Cargo pit number 4.

The hole was examined closely. The metal was bent outward. The fuselage near it was burned and discolored. And, since there were no gas lines or tanks in that area of the plane, the conclusion was evident: there had been a violent explosion aboard.

About 100 agents were then sent across the nation to learn all about the passengers and crew—as well as their bags. They quickly ruled out the possibility of an accidental explosion in a suitcase or piece of cargo.

One passenger's luggage, though, yielded some clues. The handbag of Mrs. Daisie King contained a newspaper article that said her son—Jack Graham—was wanted for forgery. Hmmm. And, just a few scraps were all that was left of another piece of her luggage. Soon, agents unraveled the whole story—Graham's criminal past, his dysfunctional relationship with his mother, and his purchase of explosives and the insurance policies. When confronted, Graham confessed. He later recanted, but the evidence was overwhelming. He was convicted at trial.

The case helped lay the groundwork for even more complex airline disasters down the road—including the downing of Pan Am Flight 103 by a terrorist bomb in Scotland in 1988.

**Left: The wreckage of the plane was carefully laid out in a Denver warehouse, helping investigators solve the case.
Above: The tail of the plane was discovered on a Colorado farm.**

FAMOUS CASES

An Odd Couple of Crime

The days of the big-name bank robbers—John Dillinger, "Baby Face" Nelson, "Pretty Boy" Floyd, and the like—were long gone when a pair of enterprising, dangerous, and slightly offbeat crooks arrived on the scene in the early 1960s. But within a few years, they'd be as wanted as any of the gun-slinging bank robbers of the gangster era.

Their names were Albert Nussbaum and Bobby Wilcoxson, and before they were locked away for good, they'd robbed eight banks, accumulated a massive arsenal of weapons, murdered a bank guard, and set off several bombs in the nation's capital.

Albert Nussbaum

The two men were a study in contrasts. Nussbaum was quiet and clever, a thinker and a planner. He was a student of crime, devouring books on explosives, electronics, criminal investigations, and firearms. An entrepreneur of sorts, he used his ill-gotten gains to set up several companies. He was the "brains" of the pair. Wilcoxson, on the other hand, supplied the "brawn." During their robberies, he was the one barking orders and brandishing the heavy weapons.

Bobby Wilcoxson

The two had become friends in an Ohio prison and hooked up after they were released. They robbed their first bank in Buffalo in December 1960, with Wilcoxson wielding a sawed-off shotgun that Nussbaum had cleverly hidden under his partner's winter coat by drilling a hole in the barrel and tying it around Wilcoxson's shoulder with a shoelace.

In June 1961, they made their first big mistake. Nussbaum built his own homemade bombs, which he planned to use to distract law enforcement while the two robbed a bank in Washington, D.C. They set off two test bombs successfully, sending the police scrambling. But the third bomb failed to detonate, and the FBI lifted Nussbaum's fingerprints from it. Still, the pair went ahead and robbed the bank anyway.

It was their fifth robbery in December 1961 that put them on the Bureau's "Top Ten" fugitive list. Desperate for money, Nussbaum and Wilcoxson cased a bank in Brooklyn, but realized that they'd have to knock off the bank guard to make it work. Their plan—which included a new recruit named Peter Curry—went horribly awry. After Wilcoxson killed the guard with four blasts

from his Thompson submachine gun, a fleeing customer alerted police. Wilcoxson got into a gun battle with one officer, who was wounded but survived. All three criminals got away, barely, but Curry was arrested within two months. He told agents what he knew about Nussbaum and Wilcoxson and led them to the countryside in Buffalo, where the pair had hidden a massive cache of weapons.

At that point, the search heated up. The two men, along with Wilcoxson's girlfriend Jackie Rose, became national fugitives and were forced into hiding. They began using aliases and wearing disguises. Still, they committed three more robberies.

In the end, the two men had a falling out and went their separate ways. Nussbaum contacted his estranged wife in desperation. Her mother called the FBI, and the wife reluctantly agreed to help catch him. Following a wild car chase, agents arrested Nussbaum on November 4, 1962. They caught up with Wilcoxson and Rose, living together with their young child, six days later.

Both Nussbaum and Wilcoxson ultimately pled guilty. In February 1964, they were sentenced to life in prison. The FBI's search, which involved every one of its field offices and many countries around the world, was over. And a crime partnership that began in prison ended there, with the two men bitter enemies.

Top: The homemade bomb built by Nussbaum that failed to detonate
Bottom: Wilcoxson brandishes a gun during the Brooklyn robbery

FAMOUS CASES

The Baptist Church Bombing

It was a quiet Sunday morning in Birmingham, Alabama—around 10:24 on September 15, 1963—when a dynamite bomb exploded in the back stairwell of the downtown Sixteenth Street Baptist Church. The violent blast ripped through the wall, killing four African-American girls on the other side and injuring more than 20 inside the church.

It was a clear act of racial hatred: the church was a key civil rights meeting place and had been a frequent target of bomb threats.

The FBI office in Birmingham launched an immediate investigation and wired Director Hoover about the crime. FBI bomb experts raced to the scene—via military jet—and a dozen more personnel from other offices were sent to assist Birmingham.

At 10:00 p.m. that night, FBI Assistant Director Al Rosen assured Deputy Attorney General Nicholas Katzenbach that "the Bureau considered this a most heinous offense … [and] … we had entered the investigation with no holds barred."

And the Bureau backed up its promise. Dozens of FBI agents—as many as 36 at one point—worked the case throughout September and October and into the next year. One internal memo noted that:

The Sixteenth Street Baptist Church before the bombing

"…We have practically torn Birmingham apart and have interviewed thousands of persons. We have seriously disrupted Klan activities by our pressure and interviews so that these organizations have lost members and support. …We have made extensive use of the polygraph, surveillances, microphone surveillances and technical surveillances…"

By 1965, the Bureau had serious suspects—namely, Robert E. Chambliss, Bobby Frank Cherry, Herman Frank Cash, and Thomas E. Blanton, Jr., all KKK members—but witnesses were reluctant to talk and physical evidence was lacking. Also, at that time, information from surveillances was not admissible in court. As a result, no federal charges were filed in the '60s and the case was closed.

It has been claimed that Director Hoover held back evidence from prosecutors in the '60s or even tried to block prosecution. It's simply not true. His concern was to prevent leaks, not to stifle justice. In one memo concerning a Justice Department prosecutor seeking information, he wrote, "Haven't these reports already been furnished to the Dept.?" In 1966, Hoover overruled his staff and made transcripts of wiretaps available to Justice.

In the end, justice was served. Chambliss received life in prison in 1977 following a case led by Alabama Attorney General Robert Baxley. And eventually the fear, prejudice, and reticence that kept witnesses from coming forward began to subside. The FBI re-opened the case in the mid-1990s, and Blanton and Cherry were indicted in May 2000. Both were convicted at trial and sentenced to life in prison. The fourth man, Herman Frank Cash, had died in 1994.

The force of the blast was so powerful that it blew a hole in the back of the church and shattered windows across the street.

FAMOUS CASES

Mississippi Burning

The KKK was in a murderous mood. It was June 1964—the start of "Freedom Summer," a massive three-month initiative to register southern blacks to vote and a direct response to the Klan's own campaign of fear and intimidation.

The Klan in Mississippi, in particular, was after a 24-year-old New Yorker named Michael Schwerner. He'd been especially active in organizing local boycotts of biased businesses and helping with voter registration. On June 16, acting on a tip, a mob of armed KKK members descended on a local church meeting looking for him. Schwerner wasn't there, so they torched the church and beat the churchgoers.

Michael Schwerner

The Klan missed its target, but the trap was set: on June 20, Schwerner and two fellow volunteers—James Chaney and Andrew Goodman—headed south to investigate the fire. The next afternoon, they interviewed several witnesses and went to meet with fellow activists. The events that followed, outlined here, would stun the nation.

James Chaney

5 p.m., Sunday, June 21: After driving into Philadelphia, Mississippi, the three civil rights workers were arrested by a Neshoba County Deputy Sheriff named Cecil Price, allegedly for speeding.

Circa 10:30 p.m., June 21: Chaney, Goodman, and Schwerner were released and drove off in the direction of Meridian in their blue station wagon. By preordained plan, KKK members followed. The activists were never heard from again.

Andrew Goodman

Early morning, June 22: Notified of the disappearance, the Department of Justice requested the FBI's involvement; a few hours later, Attorney General Robert Kennedy asked the Bureau to lead the case. By late morning, FBI agents blanketed the area and began intensive interviews.

Late afternoon, June 23: Intelligence developed by agents led them to the remains of the burnt-out station wagon. No bodies were found; the worst was feared. The charred station wagon led agents to name the case "MIBURN," for Mississippi Burning.

June 24 to August 3: Agents launched a massive search for the young men—aided by the National Guard—through back roads, swamps, and hollows. At the same time, investigators were putting pressure on known KKK members and developing informants who could infiltrate the Klan. At the request of President Lyndon Johnson, the Bureau also opened a new field office in Jackson, Mississippi. In time, agents had developed a comprehensive analysis of the local KKK and its role in the disappearance.

August 4: Acting on an informant tip, the Bureau found all three bodies buried 14 feet below an earthen dam on a local farm.

December 4: More than a dozen suspects, including Deputy Sheriff Price and his boss, Sheriff Rainey, were indicted and arrested.

October 20, 1967: Following years of court battles, seven of the 18 defendants were found guilty—including Deputy Sheriff Price—but none on murder charges. One major conspirator, Edgar Ray Killen, went free after a lone juror couldn't bring herself to convict a Baptist preacher.

In the end, the Klan's homicidal ways backfired. The murders galvanized the nation and provided impetus for the passage of the landmark Civil Rights Act of 1964 on July 2. And Killen eventually got his due; he was convicted of manslaughter on June 21, 2005, the 41st anniversary of the crimes.

Above: Agents digging up the remains of the three murdered civil rights workers
Below: This charred station wagon led agents to name the case "MIBURN," for "Mississippi Burning."

FAMOUS CASES

Assassination, Times Three

RFK, JFK, and MLK—each gunned down by lone assassins in the span of five years. Or were these high-profile murders part of larger conspiracies? Many questions have been raised...

Lee Harvey Oswald

First: Who shot President Kennedy? Were the Mafia or Fidel Castro or the KGB or LBJ or even the FBI and CIA behind his very visible murder in Dealey Plaza on November 22, 1963? Could Lee Harvey Oswald have fired so many shots in just a few seconds? What about the smoke and suspicious characters on the "Grassy Knoll"? Who were the three clean-shaven "tramps" found in a nearby rail yard right soon after the shooting? Was Jack Ruby trying to silence Oswald?

James Earl Ray

Second: Did James Earl Ray really fire the shot that killed Dr. Martin Luther King on the balcony of a Memphis motel on April 4, 1968? Ray, after all, wasn't a trained sniper. Maybe Memphis barman Lloyd Jowers was involved, hiring a hit man to carry out the killing. Or maybe that mysterious man named "Raoul" or "Raul" (later said to be a retired auto worker in New York) was behind the whole thing, framing the hapless Ray. Or maybe it was the Mafia (again) or the FBI (again) or even the Green Berets.

Sirhan Sirhan

Third: What of the murder of the campaigning Senator Robert Kennedy in the Ambassador Hotel in Los Angeles in June 1968? A Palestinian Arab named Sirhan Sirhan was nabbed by police moments after shots were fired in the hotel kitchen. But was he acting alone? Who was that mystery woman in a polka-dot dress who supposedly met with Sirhan the night before? Did L.A. police destroy some of the ballistic evidence? Were witnesses pressured to change their stories? Was the CIA somehow involved?

The FBI story: Questions often abound after high-profile murders, and criminal cases are rarely wrapped up as cleanly as they are in books and the movies. But the FBI-led investigations—among the most thorough ever conducted by the Bureau—found no evidence of conspiracies in any of the assassinations.

JFK: After conducting some 25,000 interviews and running down tens of thousands of investigative leads, the FBI found that Lee Harvey Oswald acted alone. The Warren Commission, which spent nearly a year carefully studying the assassination, agreed. Fifteen years later, the House Select Committee on Assassina-

tions still wondered whether Oswald had help but concluded that the FBI had conducted a "thorough and professional investigation" and was certainly not involved in the shooting.

MLK: James Earl Ray was a known racist, with a criminal record as long as your arm. The FBI found his fingerprints on a rifle near the crime scene and in a car seen in the area. Agents determined that Ray had purchased a rifle in Alabama and rented a room in Memphis near the hotel where Dr. King was shot. Shortly after the murder, Ray fled the country; the Bureau later tracked him down in London. He initially confessed to the killing, although he later recanted. A final report issued by the House Select Committee on Assassinations in 1979 concluded that Ray was the lone shooter.

RFK: During Sirhan's trial, his lawyers didn't dispute that their client shot Kennedy, instead arguing that he was insane. Sirhan was found guilty of first-degree murder in April 1969. In 1992, a Los Angeles County grand jury refused to reopen the case following claims of new evidence and a police cover-up.

The cases, at least for the moment, are closed.

President John Kennedy

Senator Robert Kennedy

Dr. Martin Luther King, Jr.

FAMOUS CASES

The D.B. Cooper Mystery

On the afternoon of November 24, 1971, a non-descript man calling himself Dan Cooper approached the counter of Northwest Orient Airlines in Portland, Oregon. He used cash to buy a one-way ticket on Flight 305, bound for Seattle, Washington. Thus began one of the great unsolved mysteries in FBI history.

Cooper was a quiet man who appeared to be in his mid-40s, wearing a business suit with a black tie and white shirt. He ordered a drink—bourbon and soda—while the flight was waiting to take off. A short time after 3:00 p.m., he handed the stewardess a note indicating that he had a bomb in his briefcase and wanted her to sit with him.

The stunned stewardess did as she was told. Opening a cheap attaché case, Cooper showed her a glimpse of a mass of wires and red colored sticks and demanded that she write down what he told her. Soon, she was walking a new note to the captain of the plane that demanded four parachutes and $200,000 in $20 bills.

When the flight landed in Seattle, the hijacker exchanged the flight's 36 passengers for the money and parachutes. Cooper kept several crew members, and as the plane took off again, he ordered the pilot to set a course for Mexico City.

Somewhere between Seattle and Reno, shortly after 8:00 p.m., the hijacker did the incredible: he jumped out of the back of the plane with a parachute and the ransom money. The pilots landed safely, but Cooper had disappeared into the night and his ultimate fate remains a mystery to this day.

The FBI learned of the crime in progress and immediately opened an extensive investigation that lasted many years. Calling it NORJAK, for Northwest hijacking, agents interviewed hundreds of people, tracked leads across the nation, and scoured the aircraft for evidence. By the five-year anniversary of the hijacking, the Bureau had considered more than 800 suspects and eliminated all but two dozen from consideration.

One person on the list, Richard Floyd McCoy, is still a favorite suspect for many. Agents tracked down and arrested McCoy for a similar airplane hijacking and parachute escape less than five months after Cooper's flight. But McCoy was later ruled out because he didn't match the nearly identical physical descriptions of Cooper provided by flight attendants and for other reasons.

It's likely that Cooper didn't survive his jump from the plane. After all, the parachute he used couldn't be steered, his shoes

Left: FBI rendition of "D.B." Cooper.

and clothing were unsuitable for a rough landing, and he jumped into a wooded area at night, a dangerous proposition even for a seasoned pro—which evidence suggests Cooper was not. This theory was given a boost in 1980 when a young boy found a rotting package full of $20 bills ($5,800 in all) that matched the serial numbers of the money stolen by Cooper.

Where did "D.B." come from? It was apparently a myth created by the press. Agents did question a man with the initials "D. B." but he wasn't the hijacker.

The daring hijack and disappearance remain an intriguing mystery—for law enforcement and amateur sleuths alike. In 2007, the case was reignited—thanks to a Seattle special agent and new technologies like DNA testing, which helped rule out at least one suspect. The agent provided a series of pictures and information to the public in the hopes that it might jog someone's memory or provide new leads. After all these years, the FBI would still like to get its man.

Top: Some of the missing money that was recovered by a young boy in 1980
Bottom: One of the parachutes requested but never used by Cooper.

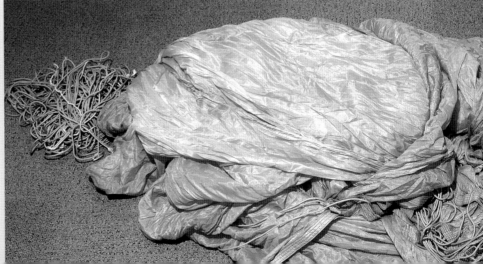

Crime and Corruption Across America, *1972-1988*

A night guard at the Watergate Complex was making his rounds early one Saturday morning when he came across an exit door that had been taped open. He was immediately suspicious.

It was June 17, 1972, and he'd just uncovered what would become the most famous burglary in U.S. history.

Five men were arrested by police a few minutes later for breaking into the Democratic National Committee Headquarters inside the Watergate. Police also found fake IDs, bugging equipment, and lookouts in the motel across the street.

Things snowballed from there. President Richard Nixon's reelection campaign had not only been caught committing an illegal political dirty trick, but the administration reacted by lying and covering up the crime and others. Two years later, President Nixon resigned rather than face certain impeachment.

From the moment that police realized the Watergate break-in was no ordinary burglary, the FBI was on the case. But the timing couldn't have been worse. It had been less than five weeks since J. Edgar Hoover—the only Director FBI employees had known—had died in his sleep. For years, criticism of the Bureau and Hoover had been building. There was dissatisfaction with Hoover's age, increasing political disagreement over the Bureau's tactics and techniques, and widespread unease over the chaos and violence of the late 1960s.

Acting FBI Director L. Patrick Gray testifies Now, the FBI was about to become involved in the most politically sensitive investigation in its history.

During the Watergate scandal, the FBI faced political pressure from the White House and even from within its own walls— Acting Director L. Patrick Gray was accused of being too pli-

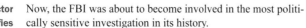

May 3, 1972
L. Patrick Gray named Acting Director upon death of J. Edgar Hoover

May 8, 1972
New, modern FBI Academy training facility opened at Quantico, Virginia

The Watergate Complex. The break-ins occured in the office building in the center.

able to White House demands and resigned on April 27, 1973. And throughout, a high-ranking official—dubbed "Deep Throat" and ultimately identified in 2005 as FBI Deputy Director Mark Felt—was leaking investigative information to the press.

Still, FBI agents diligently investigated the crime and traced its hidden roots, working closely with the special prosecutor's office created by the Attorney General and with the Senate Select Committee on Presidential Campaign Activities. Nearly every Bureau field office was involved in the case. Agents prepared countless reports and conducted some 2,600 interviews requested by the special prosecutor. The FBI Laboratory and Identification Division also lent their services. In the end, the Bureau's contributions to unraveling the Watergate saga were invaluable.

In the midst of Watergate, the Bureau had gained new leadership. Clarence Kelley, a former FBI agent and Kansas City,

Missouri, Chief of Police, took office on July 9, 1973. Kelley had the tough task of moving the FBI into the post-Hoover era. He did an admirable job of restoring public trust in the agency, frankly admitting that mistakes had been made and leading a number of far-reaching and necessary reforms.

In response to criticism of the Bureau's Cointelpro operation (see page 57), for example, he reorganized FBI intelligence efforts. In February 1973, the General Investigations Division took over responsibility for investigating domestic terrorists and subversives, working under more strict guidelines and limiting its efforts to actual criminal violations. The Intelligence Division retained foreign counterintel-

FBI Deputy Director Mark Felt, who later admitted to being "Deep Throat"

July 9, 1973
Clarence Kelley sworn in as Director

February 4, 1974
Patty Hearst kidnapped by Symbionese Liberation Army

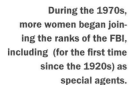

ligence responsibilities but was renamed the National Security Division.

Kelley's most significant management innovation was shifting the FBI's longstanding investigative focus from "quantity" to "quality," directing each field office to set priorities based on the most important threats in its territory and to concentrate their resources on those issues.

And what were those threats? During the 1970s, domestic terrorism and foreign intrigue remained key concerns, as the radical unrest of the 1960s had spilled into the next decade and the Cold War was still raging. The FBI had its hands full with homegrown terrorist groups like the Symbionese Liberation Army—which wanted to lead a violent revolution against the U.S. government and kidnapped newspaper heiress Patty Hearst to help its cause (see page 74)—and the Weather Underground (see page 75), which conducted a campaign of bombings that targeted everything from police stations to the Pentagon. And spy cases still abounded—from the "Falcon and the Snowman" investigation that uncovered two former altar boys from wealthy

June 26, 1975
Special Agents Jack Coler and Ronald Williams slain near Pine Ridge, South Dakota

The FBI Academy at Quantico

In 1972, today's FBI Academy—which trains not only Bureau personnel but also law enforcement professionals from around the globe—opened its doors on a sprawling 385-acre campus carved out of the Quantico Marine Corps base in rural Virginia.

How did the Bureau end up at Quantico? It all started in 1934, when Congress gave agents the authority to carry firearms and make arrests. The Bureau needed a safe, out-of-the-way place to learn marksmanship and to take target practice. The U.S. Marine Corps was ready to help, loaning a firing range at its base in Quantico, about 35 miles southwest of Washington, D.C.

By the late 1930s, the FBI needed a central place to instruct and house the growing number of police officers and special agents it was training, along with a range that met the Bureau's more specialized law enforcement work. So in 1939, the Marine Corps loaned the Bureau land to build its own training facility and firing range. The first FBI classroom building opened on the main section of the base in 1940. The FBI Academy was born.

Over the next two decades, the FBI added to the original building. But it still wasn't enough. Eight people shared a single dorm room. The lack of classroom space limited the size of training classes. The firing range was a bumpy bus ride away. The FBI needed the facilities to match its vision for world-class training. In 1965, the FBI got approval to build a brand new complex at Quantico. The Marine Corps obliged once again, loaning more acres on the outskirts of the base.

On May 7, 1972, the new, expanded, and modernized FBI Academy was opened. Talk about a major upgrade: the complex included more than two dozen classrooms, eight conference rooms, twin seven-story dormitories, a 1,000-seat auditorium, a dining hall, a full-sized gym and swimming pool, a fully equipped library, and new firing ranges. Not to mention much-needed enhancements like specialized classrooms for forensic science training, four identification labs, more than a dozen darkrooms, and a simulated-city and crime scene room for practical exercises.

Since 1972, the Academy has continued to grow and evolve, both in terms of its training and its facilities. In 1976, the FBI created the National Executive Institute for the heads of the nation's largest law enforcement agencies. More leadership training programs have followed. In 1987, the Bureau built a mock town on campus called "Hogan's Alley," providing a realistic training ground for agents.

Joining the Academy complex in the 1980s and 1990s were the Engineering Research Facility and the Critical Incident Re-

Above: An aerial view of the FBI Academy
Left: A few buildings at "Hogan's Alley," a realistic town for training new agents built with the help of Hollywood set designers, complete with local actors playing the "bad guys" during simulated exercises

sponse Group, which includes the FBI's Hostage Rescue Team and behavioral scientists. In 2002, the FBI also launched the College of Analytical Studies—now called the Center for Intelligence Training—to develop and train its cadre of intelligence analysts. The following year, the Bureau opened its first ever standalone Laboratory building, a state-of-the-art facility that helps the FBI continue its pioneering work in forensic science.

Top: The FBI moved into its massive new Headquarters building in Washington, D.C., beginning in June 1974. Bottom: An cryptologist at the FBI Laboratory works to break codes

families selling secrets to the Soviets…to "Operation Lemon-Aid," where the FBI used a double agent to unmask Soviet diplomats working as KGB spies.

The Bureau was also increasingly turning its focus to big-time crime and corruption across the nation. For the first time, Kelley made combating organized crime and white-collar crime

national investigative priorities. And the Bureau went after them in a big way.

Organized crime was certainly nothing new in America. The Italian imported "La Cosa Nostra"—literally translated as "this thing of ours"—had come to the nation's attention in 1890, when the head of the New Orleans police department was murdered execution-style by Italian and Sicilian immigrants. In the 1930s, Charles "Lucky" Luciano had set up the modern-day La Cosa Nostra, creating the family structure (led by "dons" or "bosses") and ruling body ("the Commission") and running the entire operation like a business.

By the 1950s and 1960s, organized crime had become entrenched in many major cities, and the collective national impact was staggering. Mobsters were feeding American vices like gambling and drug use; undermining traditional institutions like labor unions and legitimate industries like construction and trash hauling; sowing fear and violence in communities; corrupting the government through graft, extortion, and intimidation; and costing the nation billions of dollars through lost jobs and tax revenues.

Though somewhat limited in its authorities, the Bureau had begun targeting mobsters early as the 1930s, using a mixture of

---

September 30, 1975
New FBI Headquarters building formally dedicated

March 10, 1976
New Attorney General guidelines issued for FBI intelligence activities

investigations and intelligence to break up mob rackets. Following revelations at Apalachin, New York (see page 53), the FBI had stepped up its efforts. By 1970, the FBI had gained some important new tools to go after mobsters—including court-authorized wiretaps, jurisdiction over mob-infiltrated businesses, and the ability to target entire crime families and their leaders instead of just bit players and isolated wise guys.

In the mid-1970s, the FBI began pioneering some tools and strategies of its own. It started turning high-level mobsters into secret informants, breaking the code of silence, or "Omerta," that had protected top Mafioso for so long. And it began using long-term undercover operations—governed by new guidelines and policies—to penetrate the inner circles of organized crime. The courageous work of undercover agents like Joe Pistone (see page 78)—who almost became a "made" Mafia member while gathering invaluable intelligence as "Donnie Brasco" for nearly six years—and of cooperating witnesses like businessman Lou Peters—whose Cadillac dealership became the basis for a long-term operation that targeted the Bonnano crime family in California—injected new energy into FBI investigations and intelligence work.

Using these strategies and tools, the Bureau started racking up unprecedented successes against organized crime. Beginning in 1975, for example, a case code-named "Unirac" (for union racketeering) broke the mob's broad stranglehold on the shipping industry, leading to more than 100 convictions. In a two-part operation launched in 1978, the FBI struck a major blow against organized crime leadership in Cleveland, Milwaukee, Chicago, Kansas City, and Las Vegas through an investigation that uncovered the mob's corrupt influence in Las Vegas and in the Teamsters Union. And in the 1980s, the groundbreaking "Commission" case led to the convictions of the heads of the five Mafia families in New York City—Bonnano, Colombo, Gambino, Genovese, and Lucchese.

The so-called "Pizza Connection" case in the 1980s was a another key organized crime success—a joint investigation conducted by the FBI, New York and New Jersey police, federal and state prosecutors, and Italian law enforcement officials that cracked an intercontinental heroin smuggling ring run by the Sicilian Mafia. This case not only proved the effectiveness of undercover agents, wiretaps, and enterprise investigations, it also highlighted the increasingly important role of cooperation with international law enforcement.

From 1981 to 1987 alone, more than 1,000 Mafia members and associates were convicted following investigations by the FBI and its partners, decimating the hierarchies of crime families in New York City, Boston, Cleveland, Denver, Kansas City, Milwaukee, St. Louis, and the state of New Jersey. The Bureau also disrupted the activities of other organized criminal groups,

tackling outlaw motorcycle gangs like Hells Angels and various Asian criminal enterprises that were beginning to take root in America.

At the same time, the FBI was tackling white-collar crime in a more systematic, comprehensive way.

The term "white-collar criminal" had been coined in 1939 by an American sociologist named Edwin Sutherland; a decade later, he defined a white-collar crime as one "committed by a person of respectability and high social status in the course of his occupation."

From the days of Charles Ponzi—whose bogus investment scheme in 1919 has been replicated thousands of times since—

FBI agents arrest a member of the New York Mafia in March 1988

February 23, 1978
William Webster becomes Director

April 3, 1978
FBI Lab pioneers use of laser technology to detect hidden crime scene fingerprints

A New Era in Domestic Intelligence

In the early 1970s, the nation began to learn about secret and sometimes questionable activities of the U.S. intelligence community—including the CIA and FBI—especially during the turbulent 1960s. In response, a Senate committee chaired by Frank Church, which later came to be known as the Church Committee, held a series of hearings in 1975 to explore the issue.

During the hearings on the FBI, the Bureau was criticized for its Cointelpro program (see page 57), its investigation of Dr. King, its surveillance techniques, and the use of FBI information by politicians.

In his testimony before the committee, Director Kelley explained that Cointelpro represented only a small fraction of the FBI's overall work. He also pointed out that the nation expected the FBI to respond vigorously to the violence and chaos of the 1960s, but that it was given few investigative guidelines by Congress. Still, the FBI recognized that it needed to reform its domestic security investigations and had already begun to do so before the hearings.

In 1976, Attorney General Edward Levi and the FBI came up with a series of guidelines on how the FBI should conduct domestic security operations. The key change: to only investigate radicals breaking the law or clearly engaging in violent activity. The reforms had an immediate and far-reaching impact: the number of FBI domestic security cases fell from over 21,000 in 1973 to just 626 by September 1976.

In 1978, partly in response to the Church Committee hearings, the Foreign Intelligence Surveillance Act, or FISA, was enacted. The law set rules for physical and electronic surveillance and the collection of foreign intelligence and established a special court to hear requests for warrants.

These changes established clearer parameters for FBI investigations and made agents more respectful than ever of the need to protect constitutional rights. At the same time, the criticism and ensuing reforms had a chilling effect on the Bureau's intelligence work in the years to come, making the FBI more cautious and more willing to strictly delineate between national security and criminal investigations.

white-collar crime has evolved into a significant national threat. Over time, more and more Americans have traded their factory and farm jobs for a seat in corporate America; by the beginning of the 21st century, some 60 percent of all workers had white-collar jobs, up from 17 percent a century earlier. White-collar crimes today include everything from anti-trust violations to bank fraud, from embezzlement to environmental crimes, from insider stock trades to health care fraud, from public corruption to property and mortgage scams. These crimes siphon billions of dollars from the pockets of the American people, hurt the economy by undercutting consumer confidence and legitimate commerce, and threaten the very health of our democracy.

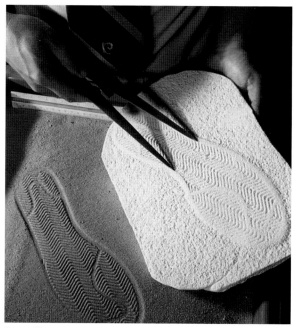

A specific shoe can be identified with an impression left at the scene of the crime by experts in the FBI Laboratory.

Among white-collar crimes, public corruption remains the most insidious. Watergate had opened the nation's eyes to the seriousness of crime in government, and the FBI became convinced that it must be a leader in addressing the problem. Using many of the same tools as in its battle against organized crime, including large-scale undercover operations, it began working to root out crookedness in government.

One major undercover operation, code-named "Abscam" (see page 77), led to the convictions of six sitting members of the U.S. Congress and several other elected officials in the early 1980s. "Operation Greylord" put 92 crooked judges, lawyers, policemen, court officers, and others behind bars in the mid-

October 3, 1980
First computerized system for searching and processing fingerprints

President Ronald Reagan right after being shot by John Hinckley on March 30, 1981. Following the attack, the FBI launched a massive investigation to determine Hinckley's motives and whether or not others were involved in the assassination attempt. Tracing Hinckley's life and movements across the country, the FBI concluded that he had acted on his own.

FBI Directors, 1973 to 1993

These three men served as directors of the Bureau of Investigation after J. Edgar Hoover died in 1972.

**Clarence M. Kelley,
1973 to 1978**

**William H. Wedster,
1978 to 1987**

**William S. Sessions,
1987 to 1993**

1980s. The "Brilab" (Bribery/Labor) investigation begun in Los Angeles in 1979 revealed how the Mafia was bribing government officials to award lucrative insurance contracts, and a major case called "Illwind," culminating in 1988, unveiled corruption in defense procurement.

Other kinds of white-collar crime began to mushroom in the 1980s. As the United States faced a financial crisis with the failures of savings and loan associations during the 1980s, for example, the FBI uncovered many instances of fraud that lay behind many of those failures. In the coming years, frauds involving health care, telemarketing, insurance, and stocks would become major crime problems.

All during this time period, the FBI also had been expanding its capabilities and technologies and integrating new responsibilities into its work.

In 1978, the same year that Judge William Webster became Director, for instance, the Bureau began using laser technology to detect nearly invisible or "latent" crime scene fingerprints. At the new, modern FBI Academy (see page 67), the Behavioral Sciences Unit pioneered work in criminal profiling—applying psychological insights to solving violent crimes (see page 73). In 1984, the National Center for the Analysis of Violent Crime was established to further this research and to provide services to local and state police in identifying suspects and predicting criminal behavior.

In 1982, the FBI was given concurrent jurisdiction with the Drug Enforcement Agency over federal anti-narcotics laws, which led to stronger liaison and division of labor in tackling the growing drug problem in America. That same year, following an explosion of terrorist incidents worldwide, Director Webster made counterterrorism the FBI's fourth national priority. The Bureau was ready: it had already begun building new partner-

January 5, 1981
Attorney General guidelines issued for FBI undercover investigations of public officials

January 28, 1982
FBI given concurrent jurisdiction with DEA over narcotics violations

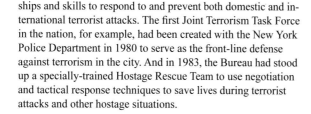

The Hostage Rescue Team, created in 1983, trains at Quantico. The team has been involved in many high-profile cases and deployed on more than 200 missions in the U.S. and abroad.

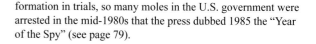

ships and skills to respond to and prevent both domestic and international terrorist attacks. The first Joint Terrorism Task Force in the nation, for example, had been created with the New York Police Department in 1980 to serve as the front-line defense against terrorism in the city. And in 1983, the Bureau had stood up a specially-trained Hostage Rescue Team to use negotiation and tactical response techniques to save lives during terrorist attacks and other hostage situations.

Director Webster also pressed for changes in the rules covering FBI national security investigations. In 1983, Attorney General William French Smith modified the guidelines for conducting intelligence investigations; the next year, Congress authorized the Bureau to pursue criminals who attacked Americans beyond our shores. That paid off quickly with the arrest of Fawaz Younis, who in 1987 became the first international terrorist to be apprehended overseas and brought back to the U.S. for trial. And with the Foreign Intelligence Surveillance Act that had been passed in 1978 and new laws that protected classified in-

formation in trials, so many moles in the U.S. government were arrested in the mid-1980s that the press dubbed 1985 the "Year of the Spy" (see page 79).

The FBI Laboratory continued to break new ground as well. By researching processes to match DNA samples obtained from evidence at a crime with samples obtained from suspects, FBI scientists contributed to a whole new field of forensic science that helps catch the guilty and free the innocent. In 1988, the FBI Lab became the first facility in the nation to perform DNA analysis for criminal investigations, and it launched a national DNA database as a pilot program three years later.

By this time, Director Webster had left the Bureau—he was asked to serve as the Director of Central Intelligence and head of the CIA in the summer of 1987. He was replaced later that year by another federal judge, William Sessions, who would oversee the Bureau as the Cold War ended and its priorities gave way to the challenges of a multi-polar, globalized world.

August 1983
Hostage Rescue Team becomes fully operational

July 10, 1984
National Center for the Analysis of Violent Crime established

November 2, 1987
William Sessions takes oath as Director

Profiling: Inside the Criminal Mind

For 16 long years, a serial bomber had been terrorizing New York City by setting off bombs in public places around town. Having exhausted every investigative angle, police turned to a Greenwich Village psychiatrist named James Brussels in 1956 for his insights into the so-called "Mad Bomber."

By analyzing the bomber's letters and targets and studying crime scene photos, Brussels came up with a profile of the bomber. It was remarkably accurate—down to the buttoned, double-breasted suit that Brussels theorized the bomber would wear. This portrait soon led police to a disgruntled power company employee named George Metesky, who immediately confessed.

From these first few modern-day steps—further developed in New York and in other cities and used in such cases as the "Boston Strangler"—the art and science of what is now called criminal profiling or behavioral analysis started to develop in a piecemeal fashion.

Special Agent Howard Teten

In the early 1970s, Special Agent Howard Teten and others in the Bureau began to apply the insights of psychological science to violent criminal behavior in a more comprehensive way. In 1972, the FBI Academy launched a Behavioral Science Unit—later called the Behavioral Analysis Unit—which began looking for patterns in the behavior of serial rapists and killers. Agents John Douglas and Robert Ressler conducted systematic interviews of serial killers like John Wayne Gacy, Ted Bundy, and Jeffrey Dahmer to gain insight into their modus operandi, motivations, and backgrounds. This collected information helped agents draw up profiles of violent criminals eluding law enforcement.

By the 1980s, the concept of criminal investigative analysis was maturing into a full-fledged investigative tool for identifying criminals and their future actions by studying their behaviors, personalities, and physical traits. Accordingly, in July 1984, the Bureau opened the National Center for the Analysis of Violent Crime (NCAVC) on the campus of the FBI Academy to provide sophisticated criminal profiling services to state and local police for the first time.

Today, the center includes several Behavioral Analysis Units and the Violent Criminal Apprehension Program, which helps law enforcement investigate and track violent serial offenders. NCAVC provides a variety of services to law enforcement and offers research into a range of crime problems—from serial arsonists to child molesters to school shooters.

Over the years, FBI behavioral experts have contributed to the hunt for the following serial killers:

- **Wayne Williams**, who preyed on African American children in Atlanta during the 1980s.

- **Andrew Phillip Cunanan**, a Top Ten Fugitive wanted for the murder of fashion designer Gianni Versace and several others in the late 1990s.

- **The D.C. Snipers**—John Allen Mohammed and Lee Boyd Malvo—who terrorized the nation's capital with random shooting for 23 days in 2002 (see page 112).

- **Dennis Rader**—aka the BTK killer, for "Bind them, Torture them, Kill them"—who murdered 10 people in Kansas between 1974 and 1991 before his arrest in 2005.

WANTED BY THE FBI
INTERSTATE FLIGHT - MURDER

THEODORE ROBERT BUNDY
DESCRIPTION

Born November 24, 1946, Burlington, Vermont (not supported by birth records); Height, 5'11" to 6'; Weight, 145 to 175 pounds; Build, slender, athletic; Hair, dark brown, collar length; Eyes, blue; Complexion, pale / sallow; Race, white; Nationality, American; Occupations, bellboy, busboy, cook's helper, dishwasher, janitor, law school student, office worker, political campaign worker, psychiatric social worker, salesman, security guard; Scars and Marks, mole on neck, scar on scalp; Social Security Number used, 533-44-4655; Remarks, occasionally stammers when upset; has worn glasses, false mustache and beard as disguise in past; left-handed; can imitate British accent; reportedly physical fitness and health enthusiast.

CRIMINAL RECORD

Bundy has been

FAMOUS CASES

The Patty Hearst Kidnapping

Around 9 o'clock in the evening on February 4, 1974, there was a knock on the door of apartment #4 at 2603 Benvenue Street in Berkeley, California. In burst a group of men and women with their guns drawn. They grabbed a surprised 19-year-old college student named Patty Hearst, beat up her fiancé, threw her in the trunk of their car and drove off.

Thus began one of the strangest cases in FBI history.

Assault rifle in hand, Hearst joins DeFreeze in robbing a San Franciso bank on April 15, 1974. It was her first crime as a professed SLA member.

Hearst, it was soon discovered, had been kidnapped by a group of armed radicals that billed themselves as the Symbionese Liberation Army, or SLA. Led by a hardened criminal named Donald DeFreeze, the SLA wanted nothing less than to incite a guerrilla war against the U.S. government and destroy what they called the "capitalist state." Their ranks included women and men, blacks and whites, and anarchists and extremists from various walks in life.

They were, in short, a band of domestic terrorists. And dangerous ones. They'd already shot two Oakland school officials with cyanide-tipped bullets, killing one and seriously wounding the other.

Why'd they snatch Hearst? To get the country's attention, primarily. Hearst was from a wealthy, powerful family; her grandfather was the newspaper magnate William Randolph Hearst. The SLA's plan worked and worked well: the kidnapping stunned the country and made front-page national news.

But the SLA had more plans for Patty Hearst. Soon after her disappearance, the SLA began releasing audiotapes demanding millions of dollars in food donations in exchange for her release. At the same time, they apparently began abusing and brainwashing their captive, hoping to turn this young heiress from the highest reaches of society into a poster child for their coming revolution.

That, too, seemed to work. On April 3, the SLA released a tape with Hearst saying that she'd joined their fight to free the oppressed and had even taken a new name. A dozen days later, she was spotted on bank surveillance cameras wielding an assault weapon during an SLA bank robbery, barking orders to bystanders and providing cover to her confederates.

Meanwhile, the FBI had launched one of the most massive, agent-intensive searches in its history to find Hearst and stop the SLA. Working with many partners, the Bureau ran down thousands of leads. But with the SLA frightening potential informants into silence, using good operational security, and relying on an organized network of safe houses, it was tough going.

A break came in Los Angeles. On May 16, two SLA members tried to steal an ammunition belt from a local store and were nearly caught. The getaway van was discovered, which led authorities to an SLA safe house. The next day, it was surrounded by L.A. police. A massive shootout ensued. The building went up in flames; six members of the SLA died in the blaze, including DeFreeze.

But where was Hearst? She and several others had escaped and began traveling around the country to avoid capture. FBI agents, though, were close behind. Hearst was finally captured in San Francisco on September 18, 1975, and charged with bank robbery and other crimes.

Her trial was as sensational as the chase. Despite claims of brainwashing, the jury found her guilty, and she was sentenced to seven years in prison. She served two years before President Carter commuted her sentence. She was later pardoned.

And the rest of the SLA? The FBI caught up with them all. The last two members were arrested in 1999 and 2002. Case closed.

The Weather Underground

"You don't need a weatherman to know which way the wind blows."
Bob Dylan

On January 29, 1975, an explosion rocked the headquarters of the U.S. State Department in Washington, D.C. No one was hurt, but the damage was extensive, impacting 20 offices on three separate floors. Hours later, another bomb was found at a military induction center in Oakland, California, and safely detonated.

A domestic terrorist group called the Weather Underground claimed responsibility for both bombs. Originally called the Weatherman or the Weathermen, a name taken from a line in a Bob Dylan song, the Weather Underground was a small, violent offshoot of Students for a Democratic Society, or SDS, a group created in the turbulent '60s to promote social change.

When SDS collapsed in 1969, the Weather Underground stepped forward, inspired by communist ideologies and embracing violence and crime as a way to protest the Vietnam War, racism, and other left-wing aims. "Our intention is to disrupt the empire ... to incapacitate it, to put pressure on the cracks," claimed the group's 1974 manifesto, *Prairie Fire*.

By the next year, the group had claimed credit for 25 bombings—including the U.S. Capitol, the Pentagon, the California Attorney General's office, and a New York City police station.

The FBI doggedly pursued these terrorists as their attacks mounted. Many members were identified, but their small numbers and guerilla tactics helped them hide under assumed identities. In 1978, the Bureau arrested five members who were plotting to bomb a politician's office. Others were captured after two policemen and a Brinks' driver were murdered in a botched armored car robbery in Nanuet, New York, in 1981.

Key to disrupting the group for good was the newly created FBI-New York Police Department anti-terrorism task force, which brought together the strengths of both organizations. The task force and others like it paved the way for today's Joint Terrorism Task Forces—now operating in each of the Bureau's field offices to fuse federal, state, and local law enforcement and intelligence resources to combat today's terrorist threats.

By the early 1990s, the Weather Underground was essentially history. Still, several of these fugitives were able to successfully hide themselves for decades, emerging only in recent years to answer for their crimes.

Three Weather Underground members were killed when a bomb they had built exploded in the basement of a townhouse in Greenwich Village on March 6, 1970. In the days following the explosion, police found 57 sticks of dynamite, four completed bombs, detonators, timing devices, and other bomb-making equipment.

FAMOUS CASES

Jonestown: Murder in the Jungle

California Congressman Leo Ryan was concerned. He'd been hearing that there was trouble in "Jonestown," the makeshift settlement carved out of the jungle of Guyana by the charismatic Jim Jones and his cult-like following called the Peoples Temple.

The allegations were serious: Jonestown sounded more like a slave camp than a religious center. There was talk of beatings, forced labor and imprisonments, the use of drugs to control behavior, suspicious deaths, and even rehearsals for a mass suicide.

Jim Jones, right, with an unidentified man at Jonestown on November 18, 1978. Shortly after taking the picture, the photographer was killed during the ambush at the airport.

Congressman Leo Ryan

In the fall of 1978, Ryan decided to visit Guyana to find out what was happening to the more than 900 members of the cult in Jonestown, many of whom were his constituents from the San Francisco area.

Ryan and his congressional delegation flew to Guyana on November 14, 1978. A few days later, they arrived in Jonestown along with various government officials and a group of reporters. There, Ryan met with Jones and interviewed many of his followers. Not surprisingly, some families and several individuals asked to leave with Ryan, who agreed to take anyone who wanted to go. Others apparently left on their own. Jones was not happy.

Fearing retribution to any left behind, Ryan wanted the entire group to fly out together, but that required a second plane and delayed the departure. As the group assembled at a local airstrip on the afternoon of the 18th and as Ryan's plane prepared to leave, a dump truck from Jonestown arrived with several armed men. They opened fire on one plane. A cultist named Larry Layton on board the other plane pulled out a gun and began shooting as well. In the melee, Ryan and several others were killed and many wounded.

Meanwhile, back at the compound, Jones was hatching an unthinkable plan. He called his followers together and essentially ordered them to swallow a fruit drink that was apparently laced with cyanide. He rationalized that the attack on the planes would bring harm to the residents of Jonestown. A few objected, but soon more than 900 cultists, including some 200 children, were lying lifeless on the ground. Jones, too, was dead, with a gunshot wound to the head.

The FBI launched an extensive investigation in concert with other agencies, with its jurisdiction based on a congressional assassination law passed six years earlier. Working with authorities in Guyana, agents interviewed survivors of the mass murder/suicide, while fingerprint and forensic experts from the Disaster Squad helped identify the many victims and Jones himself. Back home, agents fanned out across the nation, searching for and talking with members of the Peoples Temple in the U.S. for insight into the cult.

In the end, along with helping to unravel the chain of events and bring closure to grieving families, the FBI was able to make a case against Larry Layton. He was ultimately extradited, convicted, and sentenced to life in prison—the only member of the Peoples Temple tried in the U.S. for criminal acts at Jonestown.

FAMOUS CASES

The Lessons of Abscam

On February 2, 1980, the world learned of the FBI's high-level investigation into public corruption and organized crime, code-named Abscam.

The unfolding details were riveting: everything from mobsters hocking stolen paintings and fake securities in the Big Apple to politicians peddling influence in the nation's capitol. There were high-ranking government officials caught on tape stuffing wads of bribe money in their pockets and saying things like, "I've got larceny in my blood," and an FBI agent posing as a representative of a fictitious Middle Eastern sheik, gathering evidence of these big league crimes.

It all started in July 1978, when the FBI set out to catch New York City underworld figures dealing in stolen art. Undercover agents set up a bogus company in Long Island—Abdul Enterprises, Limited, thus the name "Ab(dul)scam"—said to be owned by a wealthy Arab sheik who wished to invest oil money in valuable artworks. Then, agents recruited an informant who connected them with crooks willing to sell stolen treasures. It worked. Within months, the FBI had recovered two paintings worth a combined $1 million.

Through the operation, agents were introduced to criminals who were dealing in fake stocks and bonds. This undercover work ended up halting the sale of nearly $600 million worth of fraudulent securities.

From there, the investigation led to politicians in southern New Jersey who were willing to offer bribes to get a certain "business" a gambling license in Atlantic City. Then, when undercover agents expressed interest in a suggestion to grant the sheik asylum in the U.S., these corrupt politicians arranged for the agents to meet some U.S. Congressmen in Washington who could make it happen through private legislation. For a price, of course: $50,000 up front and an extra $50,000 later.

When the dust settled, one Senator, six Congressmen, and more than a dozen other criminals and corrupt officials were arrested and found guilty.

Like many high profile, sensitive investigations, Abscam generated its share of controversy. In particular, questions were raised about whether FBI undercover efforts led to entrapment. The courts ruled otherwise, upholding all convictions. In the end, the case reaffirmed the importance of undercover operations and led to stronger rules and safeguards on these kinds of investigations within the FBI.

Many years later, the bottom line lesson of Abscam remains the same: no one is above the law. To uphold order and justice, abuse of the public trust cannot and will not be tolerated, which is exactly why the FBI continues to rank public corruption as a top investigative priority.

Caught in the act: a U.S. Congressman holds an envelope containing $50,000 that had just been passed to him by an undercover FBI agent (far left)

08-22-79   12: 43: 25

FAMOUS CASES

Undercover Agent

Dominick "Sonny Black" Napolitano just couldn't believe it.

On July 26, 1981, he and his fellow wise guys learned that Donnie Brasco—who they thought was a small-time jewelry thief and burglar, who they thought was their partner and even their friend, who they were about to officially induct into the Bonnano crime family—was actually FBI Agent Joe Pistone.

Dominick "Sonny Black" Napolitano

Pistone had fooled them all with a masterful acting job that began in 1976 and lasted nearly six years. He had appeared on the outskirts of New York City's "Little Italy" as a stranger and outsider. He slowly became known, meeting and making friends with a series of crooks and then mobsters, gaining their trust, making it look like he was participating in their life of crime—all the while secretly gathering vital intelligence on the Mafia and its criminal ways.

Carlo Gambino

It wasn't easy, to be sure. Pistone had to think, talk, and act like a crook (he spent two full weeks, for example, studying the jewelry industry). He had to know the rules of the Mafia game. He had to tell lies—lots of lies—convincingly, about who he was and what he was up to. He had to make friends with mobsters and criminals and be separated from family and friends for long stretches of time, even on holidays.

It was incredibly dangerous work as well. While playing his part, Pistone could have been seen with the wrong person or been recognized by someone he knew. His various recording devices could have been exposed or gone haywire and given him away. He could have let a word slip. The slightest mistake or accident could have cost him his life. His mission was so secret that only a handful in the FBI knew about it.

The decision to put Pistone into this undercover role was made by the FBI office in New York City, home of the five main Mafia families—Bonnano, Gambino, Colombo, Genovese, and Lucchese. In years past, the Bureau had some success in gathering intelligence on the mob, but typically only around the edges. The core—the leadership—was often untouchable because of the Mafia's code of silence. Agents in the New York office decided to try out a longer-term undercover operation—one of the first of its kind. But even they had no idea that it would end up lasting so long and bearing so much fruit.

And what an intelligence gold mine it was. The operation provided a window into the inner workings of the Mafia generally and the Bonnano family specifically (and to a lesser degree, some of the other families), not only in New York, but also in Florida, Michigan, and elsewhere. The Bureau learned firsthand who the players were, what kinds of rackets they were running, and what rules they played by. And it ultimately led to more than 100 federal convictions.

The tool that Pistone and a small band of agents bravely pioneered in the '70s was used again and again with great effect over the next three decades, generating intelligence that helped target and take down major criminal enterprises and deal a serious blow to the Mafia.

**FBI Agent Joe Pistone working undercover as "Donnie Brasco"
on the streets of New York**

FAMOUS CASES

The Year of the Spy

The Cold War was on its last gasps, but you would have never guessed it by all the moles in the U.S. government who were getting caught passing secrets to the Soviets and other countries.

It was 1985—and as a result of a string of high-profile espionage arrests by the FBI and its partners, the press dubbed it the "Year of the Spy."

Among those identified and their stories:

John Anthony Walker, Jr.
- U.S. government job: U.S. Navy Warrant Officer and communications specialist, 1967 to 1985
- Also worked for: The Soviet Union
- Secrets passed: For more than 17 years, Walker provided top cryptographic secrets to the Soviets, compromising at least one million classified messages. After retiring from the Navy, he also recruited three people with security clearances into his espionage ring: his brother Arthur, his son Michael, and his good friend Jerry Whitworth. The information passed by Walker and his confederates would have been devastating to the U.S. had the nation gone to war with the Soviets.
- How discovered: A tip from his ex-wife
- Fate: Arrested on May 20, 1985, pled guilty, and sentenced to life in prison

Jonathan Jay Pollard:
- U.S. government job: Civilian intelligence analyst at the Navy's Anti-Terrorist Alert Center in Maryland
- Also worked for: Israel
- Secrets passed: Started selling sensitive documents in 1984; the actual content has not been revealed but the quantity was significant. His wife Anne assisted him.
- How discovered: Co-workers grew suspicious
- Fate: Arrested along with his wife Anne on November 21, 1985, outside the Israeli Embassy; both pled guilty the following year, with Jonathan Pollard receiving a life sentence.

Sharon Marie Scranage:
- U.S. government job: CIA clerk stationed in Ghana
- Also worked for: Ghana
- Secrets passed: Scranage began dating Michael Soussoudis, a cousin of the Ghanaian head of state, in 1983. She provided him with CIA information, including the identity of CIA affiliates and intelligence on communications, radio, and military equipment.
- How discovered: Routine CIA polygraph raised suspicions
- Fate: Charged along with boyfriend in July 1985, pled guilty, and sentenced to five years in prison

Larry Wu-tai Chin:
- U.S. government job: Chinese language translator/intelligence officer for CIA, 1952 to 1981
- Also worked for: China
- Secrets passed: Classified documents and photographs, including CIA reports on the Far East
- How discovered: Not revealed
- Fate: Arrested on November 22, 1985; convicted at trial but committed suicide before sentencing.

Ronald William Pelton:
- U.S. government job: Communications specialist, National Security Agency
- Also worked for: The Soviet Union
- Secrets passed: Because of money problems, Pelton went to the Soviet Embassy in Washington, D.C. shortly after resigning from the National Security Agency and offered to sell secrets. Provided classified information for five years, including details on U.S. collection programs targeting the Soviets.
- How discovered: Information provided by a KGB defector
- Fate: Arrested on November 25, 1985, convicted, and sentenced to life in prison

These are just a few of the dozens of spies who the FBI identified and arrested during the 1980s, including 12 in 1984 alone. For the FBI, it wasn't the "Year of the Spy"—it was the "Decade of the Spy!"

A World of Trouble, *1989-2001*

All was calm aboard Pan Am Flight 103 as it cruised high above Scotland. At least for the moment.

It was a touch past 7 o'clock in the evening on December 21, 1988—four days before Christmas Day. The massive Boeing 747 had left Heathrow Airport in London about 35 minutes earlier on its journey to New York City. On board were 259 passengers and crew, including 180 Americans who were headed home for the holidays.

Also on board, in the cargo hold near the front of the aircraft, was a suitcase full of plastic explosives.

Suddenly, the bomb exploded with tremendous force. In a few horrifying seconds, the plane was ripped apart by the tornado-strength shock waves resulting from the blast and began plunging to earth. Not a single soul survived the attack.

Meanwhile, the southern coast of Scotland was about to become a massive crime scene. Metal hunks and fragments from the plane started raining down on the tiny town of Lockerbie and the surrounding countryside. The wing section and fuel tanks hit hardest; their high-speed impact—estimated at 500 miles an hour—wiped out a string of homes in Lockerbie, carving out a crater more than 150 feet long and creating a massive fireball that instantly incinerated 11 men, women, and children. Within minutes of the mid-air explosion, debris and human remains were scattered across some 845 square miles of Scotland.

The downing of Flight 103 was an attack of major proportions: aside from the 1983 truck bombing that killed 241 Marines in their barracks in Beruit, it took more American lives than any other terrorist strike up to that point in history. The death toll

A massive crater created in the town of Lockerbie by the crash of Pan Am Flight 103

from the incident remains the third highest from terrorism in the nation's history.

It was also a sign of things to come—a shocking prelude to a

March 24, 1989
Exxon Valdez runs aground in Alaska; FBI helps investigate

new age of international crime and terror. The investigation that followed was itself a harbinger—both massively complex and multinational in scope. The case was led by Scottish constables, British authorities, and the FBI, but it also involved police organizations in Germany, Austria, and Switzerland and intelligence agencies from many of these countries. Investigators turned up tiny bomb fragments that eventually pointed to a pair of Libyan intelligence operatives, who were indicted in the U.S. and Scotland and tried in the Netherlands. The chief U.S. prosecutor was none other than Robert Mueller, the future FBI director.

The FBI had been investigating international crime and working with global partners for years—including with the Canadians beginning in the late 1920s and the British starting in the late 1930s. The Bureau had set up its first international offices, or Legal Attachés, in the 1940s in Mexico City, London, Ottawa, Bogota, Paris, and Panama City, followed by Rome and Tokyo

in the 1950s. But the coming international crime wave would be of an entirely different magnitude.

It would be driven by two major forces.

First, around the same time that Pan Am Flight 103 was exploding into a million pieces, a shadowy terrorist organization was secretly starting to come together in the Middle East.

With their surprising victory over Soviet forces in Afghanistan in the late 1980s, tens of thousands of foreign mujahadeen who'd joined the struggle were brimming with confidence, wanting to advance their Islamic cause in other parts of the world. One group that congealed during this time was called "al Qaeda, or "the Base." Its leader—Usama bin Laden—was the son of a wealthy Saudi businessman and a successful merchant in his own right. After centering operations in Sudan in 1992,

A Scottish police officer searches for clues near the nose of the downed Pan Am Flight 103 on a farm outside of Lockerbie

December 1989
Engineering Research Facility opened in Quantico

Usama bin Laden

bin Laden began formulating plans to attack the West with an evolving, deadly new brand of jihad. The following year, Ramzi Yousef—a young extremist who'd trained in one of bin Laden's camps—would lead the first major Middle Eastern terrorist attack on American soil by planting a truck bomb beneath the World Trade Center (see page 95).

It was just the beginning. Bin Laden and his supporters would later move to Afghanistan, where an alliance with the Taliban government gave them a secluded safe haven for training recruits and planning attacks, more of which were just around the corner.

Second, the international landscape had begun changing in ways that didn't seem possible just a few years earlier, and the resulting shifts would have a profound impact on the state of security worldwide.

One major development came in November 1989 when the Berlin Wall crumbled, electrifying the world and helping to speed the lifting of the Iron Curtain. By 1992, the Union of Soviet Socialist Republics—the U.S.S.R.—was officially history.

With the end of the Cold War came a growing outbreak of freedom, not just in Central and Eastern Europe but across the globe. As the rigidity, repression, and control that characterized communism began giving way to the civil liberties and free markets of democracy, the world started opening up. It soon became possible to travel to more places, to trade with more countries, and to communicate more freely with more people. At the same time, technology was taking off, with more and more computers being connected into larger and larger networks until a "world wide web" was born. On the cusp of the 21st century, globalization had arrived in a powerful new way.

Along with these many changes came a fresh set of national security challenges. As borders became unsealed and the global

An FBI agent comforts a man who lost a loved one in the 1995 Oklahoma City Bombing (see page 96)

The Gangs of America

The history of street gangs in the United States is a long, sordid one—dating all the way back to colonial days. Over the past two centuries, gangs have changed and morphed in countless ways—spreading from ethnic group to ethnic group and from city to city, until they've put down roots in every state in the union; impacting neighborhoods, schools, Native American reservations, and even the military; getting their hands dirty through theft, murder, drug trafficking, and endless other crimes; and sowing plenty of violence and heartbreak along the way.

For many years, most gangs operated locally and fell under the jurisdiction of state and local authorities, but some started expanding their reach nationally and even internationally as the 20th century came to a close. By the early 1990s, the FBI had already been investigating some of these national groups, like the Crips and the Bloods, the Jamaican Posses, and various outlaw motorcycle gangs. The Bureau had established anti-gang squads in several field offices and had started using the same federal racketeering laws that proved successful in the fight against organized crime to dismantle gangs from the top down.

After conducting a number of successful multi-agency investigations—and recognizing the synergies gained through them—the Department of Justice and the FBI launched new "Safe Streets Task Forces" in 39 cities in 1992. These task forces—made up of investigators and prosecutors from all levels of law enforcement—blend the resources, information, and unique expertise of each agency. In 1993, the FBI also announced its National Gang Strategy, formalizing efforts to identify and pursue the most dangerous gangs by using federal statutes with tougher sentences and sensitive investigative techniques.

Gangs continue to evolve. Today, they are multiplying, becoming more criminally experienced, getting more entrenched in small cities and towns, and forming stronger networks across the nation and around the world. The FBI and other law enforcement agencies are evolving right along with them, adding new strategies and tools to the mix—from a new multi-agency task force that targets the especially violent gang MS-13 to a new National Gang Intelligence Center that integrates information from across law enforcement on the gangs that pose the greatest threat. The Bureau and its partners are also taking advantage of new technologies like gunshot detection sensors and a new software tool that combines mapping software with intelligence to pinpoint crime.

Meanwhile, the Safe Streets initiative is still going strong. By April 2008, the number of task forces had risen to 193, with 141 specifically dedicated to violent gangs.

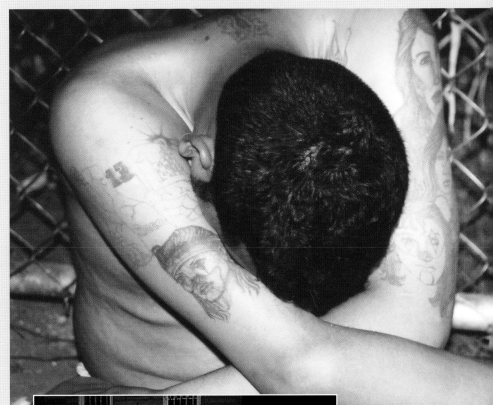

Above: An MS-13 suspect. Tattoos play a key role in gang identity and are often complex and symbolic. Tears, for example, can mean that a gang member has killed someone or has spent time in prison.
Left: The FBI arrests suspected members of MS-13

economy matured, organized criminal groups gained greater freedom to roam and conspire and found new markets for their drugs and other contraband. The threat of weapons of mass destruction falling into wrong hands was heightened by the breakup of the Soviet Union and the emergence of black markets for "loose nukes" and other weapon technologies. Competitiveness between companies and countries grew fiercer as the playing field flattened, spurring new levels of economic espionage, intellectual property rip-offs, and other crimes against businesses (in 1996 an Economic Espionage law was passed, giving the FBI a new responsibility). And technologies like the Internet gave terrorists, spies, and criminals not only a world of new targets to attack, but also the ability to attack them from the anonymity and comfort of their own crime dens.

Beginning in the early 1990s, even as it was dealing with a range of new domestic security issues—including escalating street gang violence (see page 83), major crisis situations like Waco, and the worst domestic terrorist attack in U.S. history— the FBI began reconstituting itself for a global age.

A centerpiece of that effort was new and stronger global partnerships. During the summer of 1994, Director Louis Freeh—

Waco and Ruby Ridge

Two events occurred in late 1992 and early 1993 that had a major impact on FBI policies and operations.

In August 1992, the FBI responded to the shooting death of a Deputy U.S. Marshal who had been killed at Ruby Ridge, Idaho while participating in a surveillance of federal fugitive Randall Weaver. In the course of the ensuing standoff, Weaver's wife was accidentally shot and killed by an FBI sniper.

Eight months later, at a remote compound outside Waco, Texas, FBI agents sought to end a 51-day standoff with members of a heavily armed religious sect called the Branch Davidians who had killed four ATF officers. After sending tear gas into the buildings, agents were horrified when the cultists set fire to the compound. Although some FBI agents risked their lives to save cult members, 80 Davidians died in the blaze. The loss of life was tragic, but as study after study later confirmed, the FBI fired no shots that day and did not start the fires that ultimately engulfed the compound.

Nevertheless, these two events set the stage for public and congressional inquiries into the FBI's ability to respond to crisis situations, leading to the creation of the FBI Critical Incident Response Group in 1994 that integrates the FBI's tactical and investigative expertise into a single organization. As a result of this change and the Bureau's growing negotiations skills, for example, a contentious standoff in Montana three years later was peacefully resolved.

December 1992
FBI releases first national hate crime statistics

September 1, 1993
Louis J. Freeh sworn in as FBI Director

who'd taken over the reigns of the FBI the previous year—led a delegation of high-level diplomatic and federal law enforcement officials to meet with senior officials of 11 European nations on international crime issues. A number of key agreements were hammered out and protocols signed.

The most historic one came in Moscow. On July 4, 1994—as Americans celebrated Independence Day back home—Freeh announced the opening of a new Legal Attaché in the Russian capital. FBI agents working in Moscow? It was nearly unthinkable just a few years earlier. Now, it was not only a reality but also the start of a long, productive law enforcement partnership for both countries.

The trip was just the beginning. Freeh made many more visits overseas in the years to come, sharpening joint efforts against international organized crime, drug trafficking, and terrorism. In all, he traveled to 68 countries and met with more than 2,100 foreign leaders.

He also made it a priority to open a series of new Legal Attachés, where special agents serve as official diplomatic representatives and work face-to-face with their international partners to build close, mutually beneficial relationships. As international crime and terrorism grew, these "cop-to-cop" bridges, as Freeh called them, were fast becoming vital to supporting the growing number of FBI cases with international leads, to responding quickly to crimes and terrorist attacks abroad, and to sharing

The Ones That Never Happened

International and domestic terrorists carried out some deadly and destructive attacks against the U.S. during the 1990s, both here and overseas. But did you know that the FBI and its partners prevented nearly 60 terrorist strikes during the decade, including several that could have been devastating?

Here are a few of the most significant of these preventions:

■ On June 24, 1993, following leads from the 1993 World Trade Center bombing and earlier proactive investigations by the New York Joint Terrorism Task Force, an FBI SWAT team and a NYPD bomb squad stormed a local garage and arrested a group of international extremists in the act of mixing explosives. The terrorists were planning to bomb multiple landmarks in New York City—including the United Nations building, the Holland and Lincoln tunnels, and federal building that houses the FBI's New York field office.

■ In January 1995, Filipino police responded to a fire in a Manila apartment that had been accidentally started by Abdul Murad and Ramzi Yousef, mastermind of the Trade Center bombing. A subsequent search of the apartment revealed that Yousef, his uncle Khalid Shaikh Mohammed, and others were planning a series of major attacks. Two plots involved assassinating Pope John Paul II and blowing up as many as 12 American commercial airliners flying from Asia to the United States. On February 7, 1995, Yousef was arrested in Pakistan; he was later returned to the U.S. for trial.

■ In July 1997, the FBI and state and local authorities in Texas, Colorado, and Kansas prevented an attack by right-wing extremists who wanted to engage in a firefight with United Nations troops that they believed were stationed at the U.S. Army base at Fort Hood, Texas. On July 4, FBI agents and Texas state police arrested Bradley Glover and Michael Dorsett about 40 miles from Fort Hood; subsequent searches revealed that they had stockpiled weapons, explosives, body armor, and camouflage clothing. Additional co-conspirators were arrested in the next several days.

■ On December 3, 1999, a plot to bomb two large propane tanks in California was foiled when two men affiliated with an anti-government group and outfitted with a cache of weapons and explosives were arrested by the Sacramento Joint Terrorism Task Force. A third co-conspirator was later located and detained. It is estimated that the explosion of the tanks would have resulted in widespread fire and as many as 12,000 deaths.

■ On December 14, 1999, Ahmed Ressam, a 34-year-old Algerian, was stopped at the U.S.-Canadian border with a car full of explosives. He later admitted that he was planning to bomb Los Angeles International Airport on the eve of millennium celebrations. An FBI investigation—supported by Canadian and Algerian officials and others—revealed that Ressam had attended al Qaeda training camps and was part of a terrorist cell operating in Canada.

April 19, 1995
Oklahoma City bombing kills 168 in the nation's worst domestic terrorist attack

Above: An FBI agent rakes through debris looking for clues following the car bombing of the U.S. Embassy in Kenya

Attacks in Africa

"Kenbom/Tanbom"—that's what FBI investigators called the cases of the nearly simultaneous blasts of U.S. embassies in the East African countries of Kenya and Tanzania on August 7, 1998.

More than 220 people died, including 12 Americans, and some 4,500 people were wounded. Those on the scene talked about the destruction with steel in their voices, vowing to bring those responsible to justice.

In the end, approximately 900 FBI investigators deployed to those two locations to assist in the recovery of evidence, to help identify the victims at the bomb sites, and to work with their African colleagues on the ground to track down the terrorists responsible. The extraordinary efforts of federal and international partners led to the identification, arrest, and extradition to the U.S. of four members of the al Qaeda terrorist network involved in the bombings. Each was found guilty in court and sentenced to life in prison. Several more suspects have since been arrested or killed.

The attacks were al Qaeda's deadliest prior to 9/11—but not its last. On October 12, 2000, suicide terrorists exploded a small boat alongside the USS *Cole* as it was refueling in the Yemeni port of Aden. The blast ripped a 40-foot-wide hole near the waterline of the *Cole*, killing 17 sailors and injuring many more. The extensive FBI investigation that followed helped identify the victims and ultimately determined that al Qaeda terrorists had planned and carried out the bombing.

intelligence and information to prevent threats from ever reaching U.S. shores.

In 1993, the FBI had 21 offices in U.S. embassies worldwide; within eight years that number had doubled. During that time, Legal Attachés were opened in such strategic locations as Pakistan, Egypt, Israel, Jordan, Turkey, South Korea, and Saudi Arabia. And in the years that followed, this trend continued: by May 2008, the FBI had more than 200 special agents and support staff in over 60 international offices.

During the 1990s—in case after case, from terrorist bombings to burgeoning cyber attacks—these Legal Attachés proved invaluable. For example, when al Qaeda operatives bombed U.S. Embassies in East Africa on August 7, 1998, killing hundreds of American, Kenyan, and Tanzanian citizens (see above), FBI agents stationed in Legal Attachés in South Africa and Egypt were at the scene in a matter of hours. As a result, they were able to launch joint investigations with African authorities, to preserve the crime scenes, and to gather critical evidence as life-saving efforts were underway.

These attacks were soon directly linked to bin Laden, who was indicted and placed on the FBI's Ten Most Wanted Fugitives list in June 1999. A number of top al Qaeda operatives were ultimately captured and imprisoned for their role in the bombings, and the attacks led to ramped up anti-terror efforts by the United States and by the FBI, which created its first Counterterrorism Division in 1999, consolidating its many anti-terrorism efforts and capabilities for the first time in 20 years.

During this time, joint efforts expanded with the Drug Enforcement Administration, or DEA, in battling global narcotics trafficking. In 1994, for instance, the FBI and DEA established the Southwest Border Project to focus investigative resources specifically to disrupt and dismantle the activities of significant Mexican drug trafficking organizations operating in the southwest border region of the United States. This initiative and other multi-agency operations led to the capture of several major drug lords and to the takedown of drug trafficking organizations around the world.

To further build partnerships and share skills with its counter-

June 16, 1995
International Law Enforcement Academy in Budapest, Hungary graduates its first class of law enforcement officials

1996
InfraGard begins as a pilot program in FBI Cleveland office

The mysterious mid-air explosion of TWA Flight 800 some nine miles off Long Island in July 1996 led to a long and difficult investigation. The FBI's scuba team in New York helped scour a 40-square-mile patch of the ocean floor, recovering the remains of all 230 victims and over 95 percent of the airplane. Terrorism was initially suspected as the source of the explosion, and despite a raft of speculation, a massive, 17-month investigation by the FBI's Joint Terrorism Task Force and the National Transportation Safety Board concluded that the explosion was caused by mechanical failure. Here, an FBI agent stands next to the reconstructed plane in a Navy hangar.

The Enemies Within

The Berlin Wall had crumbled. The Cold War was over. So there was no need to worry about anyone trying to steal American secrets anymore, right?

Wrong.

Turns out, the espionage threat remained as strong as ever. Instead of coming mainly from just one direction—the Soviet Union—it started to come from many places. Traditional foes were looking to rebuild their militaries and economies—at America's expense. And other nations wanted our country's secrets to help secure their place on the changing global stage... militarily, economically, or both.

Robert Hanssen

During the 1990s and into the new century, the FBI refocused its counterintelligence strategy to better reflect this new world order. That included addressing a rising threat— economic espionage. All the while, it kept catching traditional spies. Among the 50 or so people arrested for espionage during this time period were four major moles in the U.S. intelligence community who were still spying for Russia—Aldrich Ames and Harold Nicholson at the CIA and Special Agents Earl Pitts and Robert Hanssen at the FBI.

Hanssen's arrest in February 2001, in particular, led to significant changes in the way the Bureau manages its counterintelligence investigations, including more centralized oversight at FBI Headquarters. The Bureau also established and implemented a comprehensive security program focusing on personnel, information, and physical security.

Aldrich Ames is arrested by FBI agents outside his home on February 21, 1994. Ames provided a wealth of secrets to the Soviets, leading to the compromise of more than 100 U.S. intelligence operations and to the deaths of 10 American assets.

parts across the globe, especially in the fragile new democracies that had sprung up in Eastern Europe following the fall of the Soviet Union, the FBI launched a series of new international training initiatives. One groundbreaking effort was the International Law Enforcement Academy, opened in Budapest in April 1995 and led by the FBI. The academy teaches police managers from across Central and Eastern Europe cutting edge leadership skills, anti-corruption strategies, human rights, counterterrorism investigative techniques, major case management approaches, and other issues critical to building the rule of law in their countries. By April 2008, it had trained nearly 3,000 professionals from 27 nations—and spawned more International Law Enforcement Academies worldwide.

An FBI agent hunting for Eric Rudolph (inset) in the forests of North Carolina in July 1998 takes a sip of water. Rudolph, wanted for setting off bombs at the 1996 Olympic Games in Atlanta and at three other locations, was captured rummaging through a dumpster by a North Carolina police officer in May 2003.

December 8, 1997
New National DNA Index System announced

The FBI Goes to Hollywood

Whether it's the mission, the mystique, or all the suspense and drama you can wring out of catching the bad guys, the FBI has long been a fixture in American pop culture, appearing in countless movies, novels, TV shows, radio programs, pulp magazines, and even comic strips.

Among the memorable moments:

■ In 1935, Jimmy Cagney starred as the tough, smart FBI Agent Brick Davis in the movie, *G-Men*, heroically tracking down the crook that killed his friend. The film was the FBI's first appearance on the silver screen, and its huge success spawned a wave of similar movies, from *Public Hero Number One* to *The House on 92nd Street*.

■ In 1959, Jimmy Stewart played the amiable, hardworking FBI Agent Chip Hardesty in *The FBI Story*, based on a bestselling book of the same name.

■ The prime-time TV show, *The FBI*, featured Efrem Zimablist, Jr., as the iconic face of the Bureau from 1965 to 1974. The popular program, produced with the assistance of the FBI, helped recruit many new employees into the organization.

■ The tongue-in-cheek B-movie, *I Was a Zombie for the FBI*, was released in 1982 and went on to become something of a cult classic. The plot line: FBI agents work to save the planet after aliens try to turn mankind into zombies by spiking the world's favorite soft drink.

■ Starting in the late 1980s, TV became a powerful force for catching crooks thanks to popular shows like *Unsolved Mysteries* and *America's Most Wanted*, which built on the FBI's successful efforts to enlist the public's help in locating wanted fugitives and missing persons. Since it debuted in 1988, *America's Most Wanted* has helped take a thousand fugitives off the streets.

■ In 1991, the crime novel *The Silence of the Lambs* became a blockbuster on the silver screen, with Special Agent Clarice Starling (Jodie Foster) using the hot forensic science technique of the day—criminal profiling—to match wits with the brilliant, cannibalistic serial killer Dr. Hannibal Lecter (Anthony Hopkins). Several more books featuring these characters were later turned into films.

■ In 1993, David Duchovny and Gillian Anderson made their appearance as the alien-chasing FBI agents Fox Mulder and Dana Scully in the long-running cult phenomenon *The X-Files*, uttering classic lines like "the truth is out there" while hopelessly trying to find it.

■ Johnny Depp starred as New York Special Agent Joe Pistone in the 1997 film, *Donnie Brasco*, based on Pistone's memoir about his undercover work to infiltrate the Mafia (see page 78).

Today, the FBI is as popular as ever in print and on screen. Bureau sleuths are regulars on a slew of fictionalized TV dramas, including *Bones*, *Criminal Minds*, *Numb3rs*, and *Without a Trace*, and the FBI has had leading roles in many post-9/11 movies such as *The Kingdom* and *Untraceable*. These portrayals rarely show how the FBI really operates—they are fiction, after all—but the Bureau does work with many producers, screenwriters, and authors make their depictions of the FBI as realistic and accurate as possible.

FEDERAL BUREAU OF INVESTIGATION

CLARICE M. STARLING

(703) 273-0700

FBI ACADEMY
QUANTICO, VIRGINIA 22135

JACK CRAWFORD
SPECIAL AGENT

(703) 273-0700

FBI ACADEMY
QUANTICO, VIRGINIA 22135

Top: David Duchovny and Gillian Anderson, stars of *The X-Files*
Middle: John Walsh of the *America's Most Wanted* TV show
Left: Fictitious business cards of two FBI agents who starred in the thriller, *The Silence of the Lambs*

A New Home, a New Name, and a Continuing Mission

In July 1997, the Criminal Information Services Division, or CJIS, moved into new, state-of-the-art digs in Clarksburg, West Virginia. The massive complex was a major upgrade for CJIS, which had been created five years earlier from the "Ident" division set up in 1924 and from other offices.

The move came just in time to help CJIS take on new responsibilities and develop new capabilities. For example, in response to the "Brady Bill," the National Instant Criminal Background Check System was launched in November 1998, making it possible to instantly determine whether a prospective gun buyer is eligible to buy firearms and explosives—and making our nation's streets safer by keeping dangerous weapons out of wrong hands. The following year, the National Crime Information Center— a massive index that puts criminal justice information at the fingertips of law enforcement officers in their squad cars and offices—went through a major upgrade. That same year, CJIS also created the Integrated Automated Fingerprint Identification System, a national fingerprint and criminal history system that made it easier and faster for law enforcement to submit fingerprints into the database and to find matches.

Meanwhile, an era of electronic crime was coming of age. The FBI had been playing a crucial role in the investigation and prevention of computer crimes since the 1980s; the FBI Laboratory, in fact, had received its first-ever request to examine computer evidence in 1984. In 1991, the Computer Analysis and Response Team became operational, providing investigators with the technical expertise necessary to obtain evidence from the computers of suspects. Eight years later, that concept was expanded to include Regional Computer Forensics Laboratories, where the FBI works with state, local, and federal partners to gather digital evidence from computers, cell phones, video cameras, and other digital devices. By the spring of 2008, there were 14 such computer labs nationwide.

The global dimensions of cyber crime, though, became apparent as early as 1994. That summer, from deep inside the heart of Russia, a young computer wiz named Vladimir Levin robbed a bank in the U.S. without ever leaving his chair. Over a two-month period, Levin—with the help of several conspirators—hacked into Citibank computers and transferred more than $10 million to accounts around the world using a dial-up wire

transfer service. Working with Citibank and Russian authorities, FBI agents helped trace the theft back to Levin in St. Petersburg. Levin was soon lured to London and arrested.

It was just the beginning, especially as a commercially viable Internet began to take off in the mid-1990s. Computer worms and viruses had begun circulating on the Web as early as 1988, and they gained power and sophistication with each passing year. These bits of malicious code would quickly grow into a new national security and criminal threat, able to cause millions and even billions of dollars in damages around the world at lightning speed and to bring down vital military, government, and public safety networks. And before long, the Internet was spawning an increasing breed of new crime challenges—everything cyber-stalking to cyber-terrorism, from phishing to spamming and spoofing.

The FBI responded by building its investigative expertise, staffing up a series of new programs, and ultimately becoming a leader in fighting cyber crime.

November 30, 1998
National Instant Criminal Background Check System launched

July 11, 1999
Major upgrade of National Crime Information Center unveiled

For example, the Innocent Images National Initiative—which catches pedophiles using the Internet to purvey child pornography and to lure children into situations where they can be harmed—was established in Baltimore in 1995 and eventually expanded nationwide (see page 93). InfraGard, begun in Cleveland in 1996 and likewise extended across the country, unites public and private sector professionals in working to protect the nation's physical and electronic infrastructure. In 1998, the FBI's National Infrastructure Protection Center was created to monitor the spread of computer viruses, worms, and other malicious programs and to warn government and business of these dangers; this center was later folded into continuing FBI and Department of Homeland Security efforts. And in 2000, the FBI joined with the National White Collar Crime Center in standing up an Internet Fraud Complaint Center—now called the Internet Crime Complaint Center—to serve as a clearinghouse for reporting and triaging computer-related crimes and for performing analysis and research on behalf of the law enforcement community.

By the turn of the 21st century, the FBI had become a full-fledged international agency with a full plate of national security responsibilities. But the deadliest terrorist attack in U.S. history was just around the corner, and it would lead to even more sweeping changes for the FBI.

A Lesson to Remember

How seriously does the FBI take its responsibility to uphold the civil liberties of every man, woman, and child it is sworn to protect?

Seriously enough that it sends every new agent to a specialized tour of the Holocaust Museum in Washington, D.C. After the tour, agents and museum representatives talk about how the Nazis took power in Germany in 1933 with the help of civilian police and what horrors can occur when law enforcement fails to protect and serve with compassion and fairness.

The program began in April 2000 with the help of the leadership of the Anti-Defamation League, and it makes a stunning and lasting impact on the agents. The program has since been expanded to include top Bureau execs as well as police leaders training at the FBI Academy. In the mid-1990s, the FBI also began a block of instruction on law enforcement ethics for new agents and other employees.

Nestled deep in the heart of FBI Headquarters is the Bureau's high-tech command center—called the Strategic Information and Operations Center, or SIOC—which was created in 1989 to centrally manage one or more crisis situations. The center went through a major upgrade in 1998 and later became the nerve center of the FBI's massive 9/11 investigation.

FAMOUS CASES

The Mail Bomb Murders

Getting a plainly wrapped package in the mail wasn't all that surprising. It was the holidays, after all. What was inside was another matter. It was a bomb.

When Federal Appeals Judge Robert Vance opened the small brown parcel in the kitchen of his suburban Alabama home on December 16, 1989, it exploded, killing him instantly and seriously injuring his wife.

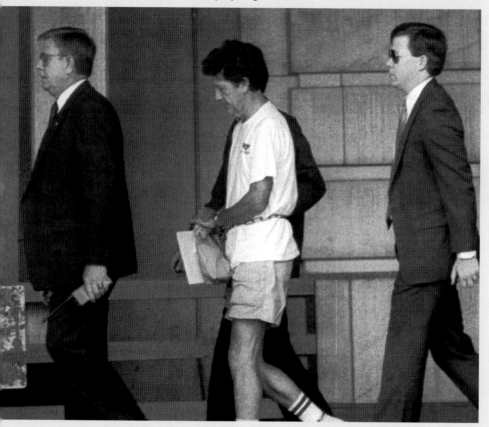

Walter Moody (center) is led into a federal courthouse in Macon, Georgia, during a hearing in 1990

Two days later, virtually the same scenario happened again. This time, the victim was Atlanta attorney Robert Robertson.

It wasn't over. Two more bombs mysteriously appeared. The third, sent to the federal courthouse in Atlanta, was intercepted and defused. A fourth was recovered and deactivated after being mailed to the Jacksonville office of the NAACP.

The murders and serial bombings stunned the nation. Who'd be spiteful enough to send mail bombs, especially during the holidays?

That's what the FBI aimed to find out. Investigators started with the obvious. Both victims were known for their work in civil rights, but that fact turned out to be a red herring.

Meanwhile, with extensive help from U.S. postal inspectors, agents gathered the remnants of the bombs and packages for the FBI Lab to analyze. They learned the path the packages had taken through the postal system and assembled a long list of suspects.

A break came when an ATF expert was contacted by a colleague who had helped defuse one of the bombs. He thought it resembled one he'd seen 17 years earlier. And he remembered the name of the person who had built it—Walter Leroy Moody.

With this lead, the Bureau and its partners began an extensive probe of the events—purchases, contacts, phone calls, etc.—and ultimately linked both the exploded and unexploded bombs to each other and to Moody. Court authorized surveillance of Moody at home and in jail (he talked to himself) provided additional evidence. Other leads were followed, suspects eliminated or linked to the crimes, and detailed analysis done on every bit of evidence, information, and trail that investigators came across.

Over the next year, Moody's motive became clear. There was a pattern of experimentation with bombs dating back to the early 1970s when Moody was convicted of possessing a bomb that had hurt his wife when it exploded. His conviction and failed appeals in that case had led him to harbor a long-festering resentment towards the court system. His contact with Judge Vance in a 1980s case led to an even deeper personal animus. The other bombs, investigators determined, were meant to throw authorities off by making them suspect that racism was involved.

By the spring of 1991, with the help of prosecutor (and future FBI Director) Louis Freeh, a solid case had been developed. The trial was difficult—Moody had made every effort to conceal his connection to the bombings. He did not succeed. On June 28, 1991, based on the extensive investigative work of the FBI, the ATF, the U.S. Postal Inspection Service, the IRS, the U.S. Marshals, the Georgia State Police, and many others, the jury found Moody guilty of more than 70 charges and sentenced him to life in prison.

FAMOUS CASES

Operation Innocent Images

In May 1993, a 10-year-old boy suddenly went missing from his neighborhood in Brentwood, Maryland. Within weeks, the investigation uncovered two pedophiles and a larger ring of online child pornographers. Within two years, it spawned a major national initiative that is now the centerpiece of the FBI's efforts to protect children from cyberspace predators.

Here's how the events unfolded: When FBI agents and Prince George's County, Maryland, police detectives went door-to-door to talk with neighbors following the boy's disappearance, they encountered a pair of suspicious men who had been "befriend-ing" local children—showering them with gifts and even taking them on vacation.

Investigators soon discovered that the men had been sexually abusing children for a quarter century. More recently, these men had moved online, setting up several private computer bulletin boards not only to "chat" with boys and set up meetings with them, but also to share images of child pornography with a larger ring of pedophiles. Both men were ultimately convicted of abus-ing children, but there was no evidence to link them to the boy's disappearance.

In the meantime, however, the original kidnapping case was expanding. Agents called every FBI office in the country to see how widespread these illicit computer techniques were. They learned that numerous complaints had been filed nationwide by irate parents who were offended by pornographic images and unsolicited obscene messages e-mailed right into their homes. Experts were consulted who confirmed this alarming new trend: sexual exploitation of children via computers.

From there, agents opened a new case in September 1994 that came to be called "Operation Innocent Images." More agents and support staff were called in. Working under strict guidelines, the agents posed undercover, pretending to be children. They en-gaged in electronic conversations with suspected pedophiles and posed as consumers to peddlers of child pornography. At times, they were stunned by the graphic images and the overt nature of the messages that flashed across their computer screens.

In the summer of 1995 the Bureau went public with the case, executing more than 100 search warrants simultaneously nation-wide. Based on this investigation, the FBI formally launched the "Innocent Images National Initiative" to crack down on illicit activities conducted through commercial and private online services and the Internet.

Today, the mission of the Innocent Images initiative is even broader: to break up entire networks and communities of online pedophiles; to take down major distributors and producers of child pornography; to stop sexual predators from using the Internet to lure children from their families; and to catch those viewing and sharing illicit images.

Much of that work is done through proactive task forces across the country, which team up FBI agents and local police of-ficers in undercover operations. In October 2004, the FBI also launched an Innocent Images International Task Force, which

brings international law enforcement officers to the U.S. to work side-by-side with agents in combating global child exploitation.

An FBI agent in the Innocent Images Unit in Calverton, Maryland, in May 2006

The accomplishments of the program are impressive: through September 2007, the FBI had opened more than 20,000 Innocent Images cases, leading to more than 6,800 convictions. And the human impact—children and families who have been protected and rescued—is incalculable.

So what happened to the missing boy whose case started it all? Tragically, he was never found. It is to him—and to the count-less victims of child sexual exploitation over the years—that the FBI's Innocent Images National Initiative is dedicated.

FAMOUS CASES

John Gotti: Making the Charges Stick

He was slippery, yes, but even the "Teflon Don" couldn't escape justice forever.

Despite the future nickname, John Gotti—a violent, ruthless mobster who'd grown up on the streets of New York—had been sent to prison several times in his early career. In 1968, for example, the FBI arrested him for his role in a plot to steal thousands of dollars worth of merchandise. Gotti went to jail, but was released in 1972.

And quickly made more trouble. Within two years, the Bureau arrested Gotti again for murder. Same story: he went to prison and was out in a few years. Soon after, he became a "made man" for the Gambino family, one of the five most powerful syndicates in the Big Apple. Gambling, loan sharking, and narcotics trafficking were his stocks in trade.

"Sammy the Bull"
Gravano

By the early 1980s, using Title III wiretaps, mob informants, and undercover agents, the FBI was beginning to get clear insight into the hierarchy and activities of the Gambino family and other Mafia families and was building strong cases against them as criminal enterprises.

The beginning of Gotti's ascent in the mob came in late 1985, when violence spilled out onto the streets of Manhattan.

The scene of the crime was Sparks' Steak House, a popular hangout for major criminals. On the evening of December 16, 1985, 70-year-old-Mafioso Paul Castellano—the apparent successor of recently deceased Gambino boss Aniello Dellacroce—was gunned down in front of the restaurant along with his number two in command, Thomas Bilotti. Gotti, who'd been watching from a car at a safe distance, had one of his men drive him by the scene to make sure his deadly orders had been carried out.

Having eliminated the competition, Gotti took over as head of the Gambino family. With his expensive suits, lavish parties, and illegal dealings, he quickly became something of a media celebrity, and the press dubbed him "The Dapper Don." Following a string of highly-publicized acquittals—helped in large part by witness intimidation and jury tampering—Gotti also earned the "Teflon Don" nickname.

FBI agents and their colleagues in the New York Police Department, though, refused to give up. With extensive court-autho-

John Gotti, the "Teflon Don," in a surveillance photo

rized electronic surveillance, diligent detective work, and the eventual cooperation of Gotti's henchman—"Sammy the Bull" Gravano—the Bureau and the NYPD built a strong case.

In December 1990, agents and NYPD detectives arrested Gotti, and he was charged with multiple counts of racketeering, extortion, jury tampering, and other crimes. This time, the judge ordered that the jurors remain anonymous, identified only by number, so no one could pressure them. And the case was airtight.

The combination worked. On April 2, 1992, Gotti was convicted on 13 counts, including for ordering the murders of Castellano and Bilotti. The head of the FBI's New York office famously remarked, "The don is covered with Velcro, and every charge stuck."

Indeed. Gotti had evaded the law for the last time. He died in prison in June 2002.

FAMOUS CASES

First Strike: Global Terror in America

On February 26, 1993, at about 17 minutes past noon, a thunderous explosion rocked lower Manhattan.

The epicenter was the parking garage beneath the World Trade Center, where a massive eruption carved out a nearly 100-foot crater several stories deep and several more high. Six people were killed almost instantly. Smoke and flames began filling the gaping wound and streaming upward into the building. Those who weren't trapped were soon pouring out of the building—many panic-stricken and covered in soot. More than a thousand people were hurt in some way—some badly, with crushed limbs.

Ramzi Yousef

Middle Eastern terrorism had arrived on American soil—with a bang.

As a small band of terrorists scurried away from the scene unnoticed, the FBI and its partners on the New York Joint Terrorism Task Force began staffing up a command center and preparing to send in a team to investigate. Their instincts told them that this was terrorism—they'd been tracking Islamic fundamentalists in the city for months and, they'd later learn, were tantalizingly close to discovering the planners of this attack. But hunches weren't enough; what was needed was definitive proof.

They'd have it soon enough. The massive investigation that followed—led by the task force, with some 700 FBI agents worldwide ultimately joining in—quickly uncovered a key bit of evidence. In the rubble investigators uncovered a vehicle identification number on a piece of wreckage that seemed suspiciously obliterated. A search of the Bureau's crime records returned a match: the number belonged to a rented van reported stolen the day before the attack. An Islamic fundamentalist named Mohammad Salameh had rented the vehicle, and on March 4, an FBI SWAT team arrested him as he tried in vain to get his $400 deposit back.

One clue led to another, and the FBI soon had in custody three more suspects—Nidal Ayyad, Mahmoud Abouhalima, and Ahmed Ajaj. Investigators also found the apartment where the bomb was built and a storage locker containing dangerous chemicals, including enough cyanide gas to wipe out a town. All four men were tried, convicted, and sentenced to life.

The shockwave from the attack continued to reverberate. Following the unfolding connections, the task force soon uncovered

a second terrorist plot to bomb a series of New York landmarks simultaneously, including the U.N. building, the Holland and Lincoln Tunnels, and the federal plaza where the FBI's office in New York is housed. On June 24, 1994, agents stormed a garage in Queens and caught several members of a terrorist cell in the act of assembling bombs.

Meanwhile, the mastermind of the World Trade Center bombing was still on the run—and up to no good. The task force learned his name—Ramzi Yousef—within weeks after the attack and discovered he was planning more attacks, including the simultaneous bombing of a dozen U.S. international flights. Yousef was captured in Pakistan in February 1995, brought back to America, and convicted along with the van driver, Eyad Ismoil. A seventh plotter, Abdul Yasin, remains at large.

Agents later learned from Yousef that his Trade Center plot was far more sinister. He wanted the bomb to topple one tower, with the collapsing debris knocking down the second. The attack turned out to be something of a deadly dress rehearsal for 9/11. With the help of Yousef's uncle, Khalid Sheikh Mohammed, al Qaeda would later return to realize Yousef's nightmarish vision.

Investigators going through the rubble following the bombing of the World Trade Center

FAMOUS CASES

The Oklahoma City Bombing

On the morning of April 19, 1995, an ex-Army soldier named Timothy McVeigh parked a rented Ryder truck in front of the Alfred P. Murrah Federal Building in downtown Oklahoma City. He was about to commit mass murder.

Inside the vehicle was a powerful bomb made out of a deadly cocktail of agricultural fertilizer, diesel fuel, and other chemicals. McVeigh got out, locked the door, and headed towards his getaway car. At precisely 9:02 a.m., the bomb exploded.

Within moments, the surrounding area looked like a war zone. A third of the building had been reduced to rubble, with many floors flattened like pancakes. Dozens of cars were incinerated and more than 300 nearby buildings were damaged or destroyed.

The human toll was still more devastating: 168 souls lost, including 19 children, with several hundred more injured. It was the deadliest act of homegrown terrorism in the nation's history.

Coming on the heels of the World Trade Center bombing in New York two years earlier, the media and many Americans immediately assumed that the attack was the handiwork of Middle Eastern terrorists. The FBI, meanwhile, quickly arrived at the scene and began supporting rescue efforts and investigating the facts. Beneath the pile of concrete and twisted steel were clues. And the FBI was determined to find them.

It didn't take long. On April 20, the rear axle of the Ryder truck was located, which yielded a vehicle identification number that was traced to a body shop in Junction City, Kansas. Employees at the shop helped the FBI put together a composite drawing of the man who had rented the van. Agents showed the drawing around town, and local hotel employees supplied a name: Tim McVeigh.

A quick call to the Bureau's Criminal Justice Information Services Division in West Virginia on April 21 led to an astonishing discovery: McVeigh was already in jail. He'd been pulled over about 80 miles north of Oklahoma City by an observant Oklahoma State Trooper who noticed a missing license plate on his yellow Mercury Marquis. McVeigh had a concealed weapon and was arrested. It was just 90 minutes after the bombing.

From there, the evidence began adding up. Agents found traces of the chemicals used in the explosion on McVeigh's clothes and a business card on which McVeigh had suspiciously scribbled, "TNT @ $5/stick, need more." They learned about McVeigh's extremist ideologies and his anger over the events at Waco two years earlier. They discovered that a friend of McVeigh's named Terry Nichols helped build the bomb and that another man—Michael Fortier—was aware of the bomb plot.

The bombing had been solved in short order, but the investigation turned out to be one of the most exhaustive in FBI history. No stone was left unturned to make sure every clue was found and all the culprits identified. By the time it was over, the Bureau had conducted more than 28,000 interviews, followed some 43,000 investigative leads, amassed three-and-a-half tons of evidence, and reviewed nearly a billion pieces of information.

In the end, the government that McVeigh hated and hoped to topple swiftly captured and convincingly convicted him.

**Above right: The devastation caused by the bomb blast
Below: FBI agents help lead Timothy McVeigh from an Oklahoma courthouse on April 21, 1995**

FAMOUS CASES
The Unabomber

How do you catch a twisted genius who aspires to be the perfect, anonymous killer—who builds untraceable bombs and delivers them to random targets, who leaves false clues to throw off authorities, who lives like a recluse in the mountains of Montana and tells no one of his secret crimes?

That was the challenge facing the FBI and its investigative partners, who spent nearly two decades hunting down this ultimate lone wolf bomber.

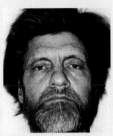

Theodore Kaczynski

The man that the world would eventually know as Theodore Kaczynski came to the FBI's attention in 1978 with the explosion of his first, primitive homemade bomb at a Chicago university. Over the next 17 years, he mailed or hand delivered a series of increasingly sophisticated bombs that killed three Americans and injured 24 more. Along the way, he sowed fear and panic, even threatening to blow up airliners in flight.

In 1979, an FBI-led task force that included the ATF and U.S. Postal Inspection Service was formed to investigate the "UNABOM" case, code-named for the UNiversity and Airline BOMbing targets involved. The task force would grow to more than 150 full time investigators, analysts, and others. In search of clues, the team made every possible forensic examination of recovered bomb components and studied the lives of victims in minute detail. These efforts proved of little use in identifying the bomber, who took pains to leave no forensic clues, building his bombs essentially from "scrap" materials available almost anywhere. And the victims, investigators later learned, were chosen randomly from library research.

Investigators felt confident that the Unabomber had been raised in Chicago and later lived in the Salt Lake City and San Francisco areas. This proved to be true. His occupation proved more elusive, with theories ranging from aircraft mechanic to scientist. Even the gender was not certain: although investigators believed the bomber was most likely male, they also investigated several female suspects.

The big break in the case came in 1995. The Unabomber sent the FBI a 35,000 word essay claiming to explain his motives and views of the ills of modern society. After much debate about the wisdom of "giving in to terrorists," FBI Director Louis Freeh and Attorney General Janet Reno approved the task

force's recommendation to publish the essay in hopes that a reader could identify the author.

After the manifesto appeared in *The Washington Post* and *The New York Times*, thousands of people suggested possible suspects. One stood out: David Kaczynski described his troubled brother Ted, who had grown up in Chicago, taught at the University of California at Berkeley (where two of the bombs had been placed), then lived for a time in Salt Lake City before settling permanently into the primitive 10' x 14' cabin that the brothers had constructed near Lincoln, Montana.

Most importantly, David provided letters and documents written by his brother. FBI linguistic analysis determined that the author of those papers and the manifesto were almost certainly the same. When combined with facts gleaned from the bombings and Kaczynski's life, that analysis provided the basis for a search warrant.

On April 3, 1996, investigators arrested Kaczynski and combed his cabin. There, they found a wealth of bomb components; 40,000 handwritten journal pages that included bomb-making experiments and descriptions of Unabomber crimes; and one live bomb, ready for mailing.

Kaczynski's reign of terror was over. His new home, following his guilty plea in January 1998: an isolated cell in a "Supermax" prison in Colorado.

Kaczynski's cabin in the woods of Montana

A New Era of National Security, 2001-2008

American Airlines Flight 11 had just left Boston and was climbing to its final flying altitude in the clear blue skies over central Massachusetts when a handful of Middle Eastern terrorists suddenly stormed the cockpit and took control of the aircraft.

It was 8:14 in the morning on September 11, 2001.

By 9:37 a.m., Flight 11 and two more hijacked planes had slammed into the twin towers of the World Trade Center and the Pentagon. By 10:03, terrorists had dive-bombed a fourth plane into a rural field in Pennsylvania after its passengers and crew heroically rebelled. By 10:30, nearly 3,000 men, women, and children had been killed—many in the most horrific of ways, in fierce fireballs and falling towers.

In the world of crime, you'd call it first-degree murder: deliberate, premeditated, cold-blooded.

The terrorist attacks that unfolded on the morning of 9/11— carried out by al Qaeda operatives under orders from Usama bin Laden—were that and much more. They were the largest mass murder in American history, a calculated slaughter of civilians, an overt act of aggression and war that took more lives and did more damage than the sneak attack at Pearl Harbor.

For the FBI—and the nation—a new era of national security had begun.

That reality was certainly clear to Robert Mueller—the newly-minted director of the FBI. He'd walked in the door on September 4, 2001 with a mandate to reform and modernize the Bureau—particularly following debacles involving FBI agent-turned-Soviet mole Robert Hanssen (see page 88), the botched Wen Ho Lee espionage investigation, and shoddy record-keeping in the Oklahoma City bombing case. But exactly one week

Two FBI agents at the site of the World Trade Center in New York on September 16, 2001

later, his job description underwent a seismic shift.

On the morning of 9/11 and in the days that followed, Mueller focused the energies of the Bureau on the unfolding, around-the-clock investigation—soon to be the largest in its history, with a quarter of all FBI agents and personnel directly involved—and more importantly, into making sure that a second wave of terrorists wasn't waiting in the wings to strike the country again.

September 4, 2001
Robert S. Mueller sworn in as Director

September 11, 2001
Simultaneous terrorist strikes in the U.S.; FBI launches massive investigation and its first Internet tip line for public leads

Left: The second hijacked airplane moments before it crashes into the south tower of the World Trade Center at 9:03 a.m.
Below: A pensive Director Mueller, who took over as FBI Director exactly one week before the 9/11 attacks

FBI Priorities

1. Protect the United States from terrorist attack
2. Protect the United States against foreign intelligence operations and espionage
3. Protect the United States against cyber-based attacks and high-technology crimes
4. Combat public corruption at all levels
5. Protect civil rights
6. Combat transnational and national c̲r̲i̲m̲i̲n̲a̲l̲ ̲o̲r̲g̲a̲n̲i̲z̲a̲t̲i̲o̲n̲s̲ and enterprises
7. Combat major white-collar crime
8. Combat significant violent crime
9. Support federal, state, local and international partners
10. Upgrade technology to successfully perform the FBI's mission

On May 29, 2002, Director Mueller announced a new set of 10 priorities for the FBI and discussed the reorganization of the Bureau in response to the 9/11 attacks.

The FBI succeeded on both counts. Agents and analysts identified the 19 hijackers within days, learned everything they could about them and the 9/11 plot, and gathered definitive proof linking the attacks to al Qaeda—all while helping to harden security vulnerabilities and prevent any further attacks.

But the Director also knew that when the dust settled, the FBI would never be the same again.

If 9/11 was a failure of imagination—as journalist Tom Friedman put it, referring to America's inability to conceive of such a horrific plot—Mueller and his top brass recognized that they would have to re-imagine the FBI for the 21st century. The Bureau's range of capabilities and its tactical response to the crime and crisis of the moment were still first rate, but the attacks showed that its strategic capabilities had to improve. The FBI needed to be more forward-leaning, more predictive, a step ahead of the next germinating threat. And most importantly, it needed to become adept at preventing terrorist attacks, not just investigating them after the fact.

The key to that new mandate, Director Mueller knew, was intelligence—the holy grail of national security work, the ability to collect and connect the dots, to know your enemies and the threats they pose inside and out, to arm everyone from leaders in the Oval Office to police officers on the street with information that enables them to stop terrorist and criminal plots before they are carried out.

The Bureau has been in the intelligence business since its earliest days. It used intelligence and intelligence-led strategies to knock out emerging threats in World War I; to dismantle Nazi and Soviet spy rings in the U.S. during World War II and the Cold War; to penetrate and take down entire organized crime families; and to head off dozens of terrorist plots before 9/11 (see page 85).

But, over the years, the FBI had often focused on making quick arrests rather than turning suspects into opportunities to collect every scrap of information about a threat…on developing comprehensive cases rather than on making prevention the overarching prime directive behind all cases. Because of long-standing neglect of information technology, the Bureau lacked the capacity to "know what it knows"—to turn all the bits of intelligence streaming in from around the world into meaningful assessments and actionable information. And it wasn't generating nearly enough quality analysis or sharing information as much as it could both inside and outside its own walls.

In the weeks and months following the attacks, all of this began to change—in a big way. Working from its own conclusions and, later, from the comprehensive reports prepared by the 9/11 Commission and other independent bodies, the FBI immediately started reshaping itself into an intelligence-driven agency and strengthening its counterterrorism operations.

The pieces soon began falling into place.

September 27, 2001
FBI releases photographs of the 19 hijackers

October 10, 2001
Most Wanted Terrorists list created

The Threat of Threats: WMD

It's what Director Mueller says keeps him awake at night: terrorists or other dangerous actors getting their hands on weapons of mass destruction—whether biological, chemical, radiological, or nuclear—and using them against the United States.

The threat is real. Al Qaeda has openly pursued WMD. And just days after 9/11, America experienced the worst biological attack in its history when letters laced with a highly potent strain of anthrax suddenly began appearing in the U.S. mail. By month's end, five Americans were dead and many more sickened. The complex FBI-led investigation—code-named "Amerithrax"—grew into a massive operation and led to scientific advances that greatly strengthened the nation's ability to prepare for and investigate biological attacks. While no arrests have been made,

the FBI's determination to solve the case remains undiminished to this day.

In July 2006, as part of its evolving response to terrorism threats, the FBI consolidated all of its WMD operations into a new Weapons of Mass Destruction Directorate within its National Security Branch.

The Directorate has since spearheaded new outreach initiatives with private industry and public partners to build awareness and encourage information sharing, including teaching companies and universities what they need to know to help prevent WMD attacks and providing them with vulnerability assessments. The Directorate has also developed proactive, multi-layered preparedness strategies with academia, government agencies, and strategic global allies and integrated intelligence into its daily work to help FBI agents and the nation as a whole to better understand and counter evolving threats.

A letter addressed to Senator Patrick Leahy being opened by experts at the Army's Ft. Detrick, Maryland, biomedical research laboratory in November 2001. The envelope and letter, which were laced with anthrax, were decontaminated and examined using a number of sophisticated scientific and forensic procedures.

Structurally, the entire counterterrorism operation was reorganized and expanded, with FBI Headquarters taking on oversight of terrorism cases nationwide to strengthen accountability and coordination with other agencies and governments. In September 2005, by presidential directive, this restructuring took another step forward with the creation of the National Security Branch, which consolidated FBI counterterrorism, counterintelligence, and intelligence responsibilities into a single "agency within an agency."

Operationally, the FBI started adding and augmenting capabilities at every turn. At the field office level, the Bureau quickly doubled and ultimately tripled the number of its multi-agency Joint Terrorism Task Forces—teams of highly-trained, passionately-committed investigators, analysts, linguists, bomb experts and others from dozens of law enforcement and intelligence agencies—mandating them to run down any and all leads and to become intelligence-gathering hubs. Back in Washington, these task forces were supported by a new National Joint Terrorism Task Force working in the heart of FBI Headquarters to cycle information among local task forces and participating agencies. The FBI also created, for the first time, a dedicated team of financial experts to follow terrorist money trails and a global command center called "Counterterrorism Watch" to assimilate and triage emerging threats and suspicious activities. And it started using sophisticated risk assessments and tracking tools to stop terrorists at the border and to track their footprints within the United States.

Technologically, the Bureau began putting sophisticated new IT tools in the hands of its agents, analysts, and other professionals—from easily searchable electronic warehouses of terrorism data to a web-based information management system that makes it easier to keep tabs on cases and share and access records. New information pipelines were also built so that the FBI could speed classified materials along to its partners.

All the while, an intelligence-driven approach was being ingrained into the FBI in important new ways.

A new Office of Intelligence—later expanded into a full-fledged Directorate of Intelligence—was created in December 2001 to lay the right foundation: to standardize policies and processes; to recruit new talent and improve training; to develop career tracks for analysts; and to create reports officers who could scrub intelligence of sources and methods and share it far and wide. Within two years, new field intelligence groups had been established in every field office to take raw information from local cases and make big-picture sense of it, to fill gaps in national cases with local information, and to share their findings and assessments as widely as possible. The growing result was that the FBI really began to flex its intelligence muscle—creating more and better analytical products, sharing information more

A robotic arm retrieves and re-files magnetic tapes containing fingerprint records at the FBI's Criminal Justice Information Services Division in West Virginia in 2002.

October 24, 2002
D.C. snipers arrested for a series of random shootings during the month

February 11, 2003
National Virtual Translation Center created by Congress to help provide timely and accurate translations

widely at all levels, connecting dots in ways it could have never done before.

One key breakthrough came at the hands of Congress and the courts. In part because of prevailing interpretations, a legal "wall" existed between intelligence and criminal investigations prior to 9/11—which kept FBI agents and analysts in the dark about the work of their own colleagues and prevented important evidence from ever reaching the courtroom. Following the attacks, thanks to new legislation and court decisions, that wall came down, and the impact has been profound. The Bureau is now free to coordinate intelligence operations and criminal cases and to use the full range of investigative tools against a suspected terrorist. The right hand now knows what the left hand is doing—an imperative for prevention.

Another imperative is partnerships. The FBI has spent a century building many positive law enforcement and intelligence-based relationships across every level of government and even across borders. Since 9/11, thanks to a new collective determination to defeat terrorism and the growing globalization of crime, these relationships are broader and deeper than ever before. They've improved at every level: with state, local, and tribal law enforcement; with foreign governments; with intelligence community partners like the CIA; with the U.S. military; and with the private sector and academia. Today, more information and intelligence is shared more freely with more partners. More agents and officers and analysts physically sit together, including in

dozens of intelligence fusion centers nationwide and in the new multi-agency National Counterterrorism Center. Joint investigations and joint task forces are the norm, especially in the U.S. and increasingly overseas, and the FBI is working alongside U.S. forces in war zones overseas for the first time in history (see page 107). Effective partnerships don't make news, but they have truly been a game changer for the FBI and its colleagues across the globe (see page 105).

The cumulative impact of all these changes and reforms has been some major operational successes in the U.S. and overseas. Sometimes by providing vital bits of intelligence, sometimes by joining dangerous raids overseas, the FBI has helped capture key al Qaeda leaders—from 9/11 mastermind Khalid Shaikh Mohammed to operations chief Abu Zubaydah—in Pakistan and elsewhere. Quite often, one terrorist has led to another and to another—yielding new streams of intelligence on terrorist threats and leads that exposed operatives and cells, some in the process of planning attacks.

Most importantly, the Bureau's work helped prevent dozens of terrorist strikes around the globe—in ways that could not always be made public. Working through its terrorism task forces, the FBI stopped homegrown plots to bomb military bases and Jewish synagogues in Los Angeles; to blow up fuel tanks at J.F.K. Airport in New York; to shoot up soldiers at Fort Dix in New Jersey; and to attack suburban malls in Illinois and Ohio. It rolled up cells in places like Buffalo, Portland, and Northern

Partnerships: The Next Generation

In this complex, globalized, post-9/11 world, the FBI's operational partnerships have never been more important to its efforts to protect the nation.

Today, the FBI works with colleagues at every level of government—local, state, tribal, federal, even international—across the law enforcement, intelligence, and first responder communities. It leads and participates in multi-agency task forces, intelligence groups and fusion centers, and public and private sector alliances. Many partners sit shoulder-to-shoulder with agents and analysts in FBI space, just as just as the Bureau shares its agents and analysts with other agencies. The FBI works on countless joint investigations—sometimes taking the lead, sometimes taking a back seat to others, sometimes contributing equally among many agencies. The Bureau's work with its colleagues is so intertwined that it's often nearly impossible to separate the contributions of one agency—and one nation—from the next.

A few examples of how the FBI's relationships have been lifted to entirely new levels since 9/11, especially in the fight against terrorism:

Law Enforcement: More than ever, local and state law enforcement is an integral part of FBI counterterrorism efforts. The FBI now provides its police partners with more and better information, such as new intelligence bulletins that detail emerging trends on terrorism and potential issues to look out for. A new FBI Office of Law Enforcement Coordination, headed by a former police chief, has built stronger relationships with national law enforcement organizations. The FBI has provided its partners with a variety of new tools and resources, too—including the Terrorist Screening Center, which enables police officers to find out right in their squad cars whether individuals they have detained have terrorist links or are wanted by the FBI for questioning.

The CIA: For the first time, the FBI and CIA are working off the same page—literally—through a common daily threat matrix that lays out every current terrorist threat and through regular briefings with other members of the intelligence community. The two agencies have integrated not only their intelligence but also their operations, swapping many more executives and analysts and even working together in a common space—symbolically, without walls—at the National Counterterrorism Center, the country's new focal point for synthesizing terrorism intelligence.

The U.S. Military: Since 9/11, the FBI has worked side-by-side with the military in theaters of war. Hundreds of FBI employees have been embedded with armed forces in Iraq and Afghanistan

on a rotating basis, working together to interview detainees, collect fingerprints and DNA samples, gather intelligence, analyze information and explosive devices, conduct raids, and secure terrorist safe houses (see page 107).

International Liaison: A new spirit of teamwork has emerged overseas since 9/11. More cases are being worked jointly, more information and intelligence is being shared, and overall cooperation is greater than ever before. Just as nations around the world have provided unprecedented support to the Bureau since the attacks, the FBI has been able to return the favor through its growing expertise—providing vital bits of intelligence that has turned up terrorists across the globe and sending teams to help investigate bombings and attacks in Pakistan, Kenya, Spain, Morocco, Indonesia, Bali, the U.K., and elsewhere.

The National Counterterrorism Center—led by the Director of National Intelligence—is the country's hub for analyzing and integrating terrorism intelligence. There, FBI agents and analysts work side-by-side with their partners from the CIA and other agencies to pool information, to analyze that data, and to draw understandings and conclusions from it. The center, established in August 2004, includes the state-of-the-art operations center shown here.

After the Storm

Hurricane Katrina was one of the strongest storms in history—and it struck the Gulf Coast with a vengeance in late August 2005. As Katrina made landfall in the city of New Orleans, the FBI stood its ground—with several agents staying behind to look after the office. The Bureau has worked ever since to help with recovery efforts and to combat the rising tide of crime and corruption that followed in the wake of the hurricane. Hours after Katrina struck, the FBI had some 500 agents and other personnel from around the country helping to secure the city, answer emergency calls, patrol the streets, conduct search and rescue operations, and identify victims. In the months that followed, the Bureau led a series of public safety initiatives to support area law enforcement and teamed up with local and federal authorities in the region and around the nation to stem the flood of scams preying on hurricane victims.

Virginia. And it helped put behind bars extremists like Richard Reid, the so-called "Shoe Bomber," who attempted to blow up an airliner in mid-flight over the Atlantic Ocean; Iyman Faris, an Ohio truck driver who was feeding information on U.S. targets to al Qaeda; and a variety of other terrorist supporters and financiers.

Even as the Bureau was making terrorism its top priority—and fundamentally changing the way it does business—its traditional criminal threats were mutating and growing in dangerous ways and demanding plenty of attention of their own. Street gangs—as destructive and violent as ever—were multiplying and migrating to new parts of the nation. Accounting shenanigans in corporate suites led to the fall of some big businesses—Enron, WorldCom, Qwest, to name a few—ringing up tens of billions of dollars in shareholder losses along the way. Public corruption, deemed the FBI's top criminal priority because it tears at the fabric of American democracy, continued to rear its ugly head, with FBI cases finding evidence of graft and greed among sitting U.S. Congressmen, state governors, and big city mayors. Even levels of violent crime, long in decline nationwide, crept upward in many cities for a few years starting in 2004.

In the days following 9/11, the FBI had to make some hard choices about resources. Its prevention and counterterrorism mandates required it to move more than a thousand agents to national security programs. This meant that the FBI had to leave some crimes—like local bank robberies, smaller ticket frauds, and certain drug investigations—to its partners.

Early on, Director Mueller decided that the Bureau's role on the criminal side of the house had to shift to targeting the largest threats—the major national and international illicit enterprises and mega-crimes that the FBI is best suited to address. Its strategy, as in counterterrorism, has been to let intelligence lead the way and to leverage the expertise of its many partners.

This strategy has been visible in just about every investigative program—from the new Law Enforcement Retail Partnership Network that tackles the burgeoning problem of organized retail theft…to the National Gang Intelligence Center that targets the most dangerous street gangs using integrated information from around the world…to the raft of new and improved cyber programs, initiatives, and multi-national alliances that tap into the collective wisdom of the public and private sectors.

December 26, 2004
Major tsunami devastates Southeast Asia; FBI called upon to help identify victims and investigate related fraud

September 12, 2005
National Security Branch created

On the Ground in Iraq and Afghanistan

Outside of its limited work following World War II, the FBI has never gathered intelligence quite like this—in war zones, working right alongside the military, scooping up everything from pocket litter to entire buildings full of seized documents.

When U.S. forces entered Afghanistan shortly after 9/11 and Iraq in March 2003, a team of FBI agents, analysts, and translators were right there with them, whether in caves or palaces, combing for terrorism information. FBI personnel seized vital documents, made a first-cut analysis of their value, and then shipped them back home for further study. Thousands of investigative leads and troves of intelligence resulted from these efforts.

In March 2005, the FBI put down official roots in Iraq, opening an office in the U.S. Embassy in Baghdad. Today, the Bureau has dozens of special agents, intelligence analysts, and other professionals in the country—one of its largest international contingents. The FBI's work there includes:

■ Interviewing suspected terrorists captured by the military for information about terrorist operatives and operations both inside and outside Iraq and possibly even in the United States;

■ Gathering intelligence, which is quickly processed, analyzed, and shared, sometimes leading to still more intelligence, creating a lightning fast real-time intel cycle;

■ Collecting evidence from crime scenes—whether from a massive car bomb or a mass grave;

■ Helping to rescue kidnapped Americans;

■ In concert with other U.S. agencies, investigating crimes committed by Americans against the Iraqi people, as well those Iraqis commit against their fellow citizens; and

■ Helping to train police and intelligence forces in Iraq.

At the invitation of the Afghanistan government, the FBI also established a Legal Attaché office in Kabul in 2005. The FBI's role in the country is primarily counterterrorism-based: interviewing members of al Qaeda and the Taliban who are captured by U.S. and international security forces and addressing terrorism leads and issues developed in the country and elsewhere.

Above left: An FBI analyst and agent in Baghdad preparing reports from intelligence gathered in Iraq
Above right: The aftermath of a car bombing in Baghdad in August 2003. The FBI helped investigate the blast and many more like it.
Lower right: Two FBI agents (left) investigate an attack on U.S. soldiers in Kuwait just prior to forces entering Iraq

In April 2003, the FBI Laboratory moved into its first standalone facility. The building, located on the campus of the FBI Training Academy in Quantico, Virginia, tripled the Lab's workspace and included new state-of-the-art technologies and equipment.

On a larger scale, the Bureau began accelerating its evolution into a single, unified law enforcement and intelligence enterprise by standardizing operations and processes in the field and integrating intelligence activities into all investigative efforts. Each Bureau field office was tasked to systematically identify threats and vulnerabilities in their domain, to proactively direct resources to collect against those threats, to quickly share information with partners locally and nationally, and to evaluate the implications of that information on the larger threat picture. Through this continuous intelligence cycle and feedback loop, the FBI has been better able to adapt itself to emerging and evolving threats.

In the seven years following the 9/11 attacks, the Bureau has come a long way. It has taken its counterterrorism capabilities to an entirely new level. It has built the strongest set of multi-agency and multi-national partnerships in its history. It has created a set of modern tools and technologies for its agents and professional staff. As a result, the FBI has become an agency that is skilled at both preventing and investigating attacks—and at using intelligence to be a step ahead of the bad guys. Despite the nearly constant adjustments the Bureau has made over the past century, the post 9/11 shift has represented one of the most dynamic transformations in the history of the FBI.

And yet, the FBI realizes that the journey is far from over. There are more improvements to make, more technologies to be rolled out, more scientific tools to be pioneered, more capabilities to be developed and refined. And if the Bureau has learned anything over the last 100 years, it is that there is always a new security threat just around the corner. In the FBI's business, there is no room for complacency.

What will the next century bring for the FBI? Only time will tell, but the men and women of the Bureau move forward building on a solid foundation—on a century's worth of innovation and leadership, on a track record of crime-fighting that is perhaps second to none. Along the way, the FBI has shown that it is resilient and adaptable, able to learn from its mistakes. It has built up a full complement of investigative and intelligence capabilities that can be applied to any threat. And it has gained plenty of experience in balancing the use of its law enforcement powers with the need to uphold the cherished rights and freedoms of the American people.

The FBI can look back proudly on a long history of protecting the people and defending the nation…and it can look confidently to the future, ready for the challenges ahead.

Protecting National Treasures

It's a small but ugly criminal specialty: trafficking in stolen works of art and priceless national treasures. And it's growing, with losses running as high as $6 billion a year. In 2004, the FBI's art specialists decided to centralize investigations and maximize resources by creating an Art Crime Team to work in major art markets around the United States. By March 2008, the team had grown to 13 agents and three Justice Department attorneys and had recovered 850 cultural objects valued at over $134 million. To enlist the public's help in locating missing cultural treasures, the FBI also launched a Top Ten Art Crimes list in November 2005.

April 16, 2007
Gunman kills 32 at Virginia Tech; FBI provides investigative support, victim services, and behavioral analysis

June 19, 2007
FBI rolls out Sentinel, new web-based case management system

Interviewing Saddam: Teasing Out the Truth

Imagine sitting across from Saddam Hussein every day for nearly seven straight months—slowly gaining his trust, getting him to spill secrets on everything from whether he gave the order to gas the Kurds (he did) to whether he really had weapons of mass destruction on the eve of war (he didn't). All the while gathering information that would ultimately be used to prosecute the deposed dictator in an Iraqi court.

Special Agent George Piro

That was the job of FBI Special Agent George Piro, who told his story on the TV news program *60 Minutes* in January 2008.

Soon after Saddam was pulled out of a spider hole on December 13, 2003, the CIA—knowing the former dictator would ultimately have to answer for his crimes against the Iraqi people—asked the FBI to debrief Hussein because of its respected work in gathering statements for court.

That's when the Bureau turned to Piro, an experienced counterterrorism investigator who was born in Beirut and speaks Arabic fluently. Piro was supported by a team of CIA analysts, as well as FBI agents, intelligence analysts, language specialists, and a behavioral profiler.

Piro knew getting Saddam to talk wouldn't be easy. He prepped by studying the former dictator's life so he could better connect with Saddam and more easily determine if he was being honest. It worked: during the first interview on January 13, 2004, Piro talked with the dictator about his four novels and Iraqi history. Hussein was impressed and asked Piro to come back.

From that day forward, everything Piro did was designed to build an emotional bond with Saddam to get him to talk truthfully. To make Hussein dependent on him and him alone, Piro became responsible for virtually every aspect of the ex-ruler's life, including his personal needs. He always treated Saddam with respect, knowing he would not respond to threats or tough tactics. As part of his plan, Piro also never told Hussein that he was an FBI field agent, instead letting him believe, for the sake of building credibility, that he was a high-level official who reported directly to the President.

It took time. Piro spent five to seven hours a day with Saddam for months, taking advantage of every small opportunity that presented itself, including listening to Hussein's poetry. Eventually, Saddam began to open up.

Among Saddam's revelations:

■ Saddam misled the world into believing that he had weapons of mass destruction in the months leading up to the war because he feared another invasion by Iran, but he did fully intend to rebuild his WMD program.

■ Saddam considered Usama bin Laden "a fanatic" and a threat who couldn't be trusted.

■ The former dictator admitted "initially miscalculating President Bush and President Bush's intentions," Piro said, thinking the war would be more like the shortened air campaign of the Gulf War.

■ Saddam never used look-alikes or body doubles as widely believed, thinking no one could really play his part.

■ Hussein made the decision to invade neighboring Kuwait in 1990 following an insulting comment by one of its emirs.

Piro was so successful at befriending Saddam that the former dictator was visibly moved when they said goodbye. "I saw him tear up," Piro said during the television interview. And for the FBI, which gathered vital intelligence and evidence along the way, it was time well spent.

An FBI agent fingerprints Saddam shortly after his capture in Iraq

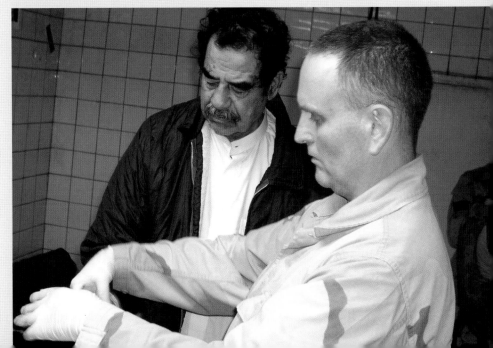

FAMOUS CASES

The Case of the Cuban Spy

Just 10 days after the attacks of 9/11, the FBI arrested a 44-year-old woman named Ana Belen Montes.

She had nothing to do with the terrorist strikes, but her arrest had everything to do with protecting the country at a time when national security was of paramount importance.

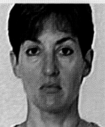

Ana Belen Montes

Montes, it turned out, was spying for the Cubans from inside the U.S. intelligence community itself—as a senior analyst with the Defense Intelligence Agency, or DIA. And she was soon to have access to classified information about America's planned invasion of Afghanistan the following month.

Montes was actually the DIA's top Cuban analyst and was known throughout the U.S. intelligence community for her expertise. Little did anyone know how much of an expert she had become…and how much she was leaking classified U.S. military information and deliberately distorting the government's views on Cuba.

It began as a classic tale of recruitment. In 1984, Montes held a clerical job at the Department of Justice in Washington. She often spoke openly against the U.S. government's policies towards Central America. Soon, her opinions caught the attention of Cuban "officials" who thought she'd be sympathetic to their cause. She met with them. Soon after, Montes agreed to help Cuba.

She knew she needed a job inside the intelligence community to do that, so she applied at DIA, a key producer of intelligence for the Pentagon. By the time she started work there in 1985, she was a fully recruited spy.

Montes was smart. To escape detection, she never removed any documents from work, electronically or in hard copy. Instead, she kept the details in her head and went home and typed them up on her laptop. Then, she transferred the information onto encrypted disks. After receiving instructions from the Cubans in code via short-wave radio, she'd meet with her handler and turn over the disks.

During her years at DIA, security officials learned about her foreign policy views and were concerned about her access to sensitive information, but they had no reason to believe she was sharing secrets. And she had passed a polygraph.

A "cheat sheet" provided by Cuban intelligence that Montes used to help her encrypt and decrypt messages to and from her handlers

Her downfall began in 1996, when an astute DIA colleague—acting on a gut feeling—reported to a security official that he felt Montes might be under the influence of Cuban intelligence. The official interviewed her, but she admitted nothing.

The security officer filed the interview away until four years later, when he learned that the FBI was working to uncover an unidentified Cuban agent operating in Washington. He contacted the Bureau with his suspicions. After a careful review of the facts, the FBI opened an investigation.

Through physical and electronic surveillance and covert searches, the FBI was able to build a case against Montes. Agents also wanted to identify her Cuban handler and were waiting for a face-to-face meeting between the two of them, which is why they held off arresting her for some time. However, outside events overtook the investigation—as a result of the 9/11 attacks, Montes was about to be assigned work related to U.S. war plans. The Bureau and DIA didn't want that to happen, so she was arrested.

What was Montes' motivation for spying? Pure ideology—she disagreed with U.S. foreign policy. Montes accepted no money for passing classified information, except for reimbursements for some expenses.

Montes, who acknowledged revealing the identities of four American undercover intelligence officers working in Cuba, pled guilty in 2002 and was sentenced to 25 years in prison.

FAMOUS CASES

Crime in the Suites: Enron

When Enron declared bankruptcy in December 2001 and took with it the nest eggs of thousands of employees and stockholders, the FBI field office in Houston assigned two agents to investigate. Within weeks, the number of agents and support staff assigned to the case grew to 45, many hand picked from field offices around the country for their expertise in traversing even the most circuitous paper trails.

The case would become the largest and most complex white-collar investigation in FBI history and spawn a unique investigative task force of prosecutors, agents, and analysts in Houston and Washington, D.C., each uniquely skilled at drilling deep into balance sheets and following the money. Their job: to learn how company officials perpetrated fraud on such a grand scale, to build a strong criminal case, and to hold accountable those responsible.

The five-year investigation led to jury convictions of top Enron officials who enriched themselves by cheating investors with sham accounting—as well as guilty pleas from some 16 others who were in on it. As a major case, it was administered at the highest levels of the FBI and the Department of Justice, as well as of the Securities and Exchange Commission. In Houston, Supervisory Special Agent Michael E. Anderson, chief of his office's economic crimes squad, led the investigation on the ground.

It all began in January 2002, when agents executed a consent search of Enron's 50-story corporate headquarters building. The search lasted nine days as investigators unearthed critical documents and emerged with more than 500 boxes of evidence. At the same time, agents conducted more than 100 interviews that helped identify fresh leads for investigators.

In February 2002, Enron's board of directors issued findings from its own internal investigation. Called the Powers Report—for William Powers Jr., head of the special investigation committee that wrote it—it said that Enron executives reaped millions by violating basic accounting principles. The report was a gold mine.

Meanwhile, agents and other experts who tease forensic evidence from computers collected over four terabytes (imagine 4,000 copies of an encyclopedia) of data, including e-mail from over 600 employees. And the Regional Computer Forensics Laboratory in Houston processed some 30 terabytes of data, helping to make still more sense of the paper trail and flagging important leads for investigators.

An FBI agent escorts former Enron CEO Ken Lay into the federal courthouse in Houston in July 2004

Financial analysts also combed through hundreds of bank and brokerage accounts to track fraudulent purchases, which proved critical in securing restraining orders, in seizing more than $168 million in assets, and in supporting insider-trading charges.

What emerged was a mosaic of interrelated schemes—some hardly more than smoke and mirrors—that toppled a company once boasting annual revenues of over $150 billion. Enron ripped off California, selling energy to the state's strapped utilities at over-inflated rates. Officials overstated the company's fledgling broadband venture, hitching the company's stock price to the star of the still-nascent Internet bubble. The company overvalued its international assets by billions to generate cash flow and manipulated its quarterly earnings statements to keep Wall Street happy and its stock price afloat.

Anderson said it was the thousands of victims—hard-working employees who lost their pensions—and the desire to hold accountable those responsible for the failure of Enron, that motivated agents, analysts, and others to press ahead on the massive case. "If it's some consolation to them, the people that were responsible for this fraud were punished for it," he said.

FAMOUS CASES

The Beltway Snipers

At 3:19 in the morning on October 24, 2002, the FBI and its partners closed in on the snipers who had been terrorizing the Washington, D.C. area over the course of 23 long days.

During the month, 10 people had been randomly gunned down and three critically injured while going about their everyday lives—mowing the lawn, pumping gas, shopping, reading a book. Among the victims was FBI intelligence analyst Linda Franklin, who was felled by a single bullet while leaving a home improvement store in Virginia with her husband.

The massive investigation into the sniper attacks was led by the Montgomery County Police Department in Maryland, with the FBI and many other law enforcement agencies playing a supporting role.

Within days of the first shooting, the FBI had some 400 agents around the country working the case. The Bureau set up a toll-free number to collect tips from the public, with teams of new agents in training helping to work the hotline. FBI evidence experts were asked to digitally map many of the evolving crime scenes, and its behavioral analysts helped prepare a criminal profile for investigators. Agents also set up a Joint Operations Center to help Montgomery County investigators run the case.

But the big break in the case, ironically, had come from the snipers themselves.

On October 17, a caller claiming to be the sniper phoned in to say, in a bit of an investigative tease, that he was responsible for the murder of two women (actually, one survived) during the robbery of a liquor store in Alabama a month earlier.

Investigators soon learned that a crime similar to the one de-

The snipers used this cut-out hole in the trunk of their car to shoot their victims.

scribed in the call had indeed taken place—and that fingerprint and ballistic evidence were available from the case. An agent from the FBI office in Mobile gathered that evidence and quickly flew to Washington, D.C., arriving Monday evening, October 21. While ATF handled the ballistic evidence, an agent took the fingerprint evidence to the FBI Laboratory (then located at FBI Headquarters).

The following morning, the Bureau's fingerprint database produced a match—a magazine dropped at the crime scene bore the fingerprints of Lee Boyd Malvo, whose prints were on record from a previous arrest in Washington State. The arrest record provided another important lead, mentioning a man named John Allen Muhammad. An FBI agent from Tacoma recognized the name from a tip called into that office on the case.

Investigators soon learned that Muhammad had a Bushmaster .223 rifle in his possession, a federal violation since he'd been served with a restraining order to stay away from his ex-wife. That led to charges being filed. And with Malvo clearly connected, the FBI and ATF jointly obtained a federal material witness warrant for him. The legal papers were now ready.

Meanwhile, on October 22, the FBI discovered that Muhammad had registered a blue Chevy Caprice with the license plate NDA-21Z in New Jersey. That description was given to the news media and shared far and wide, leading to the eventual capture of Muhammad and Malvo two days later in a Maryland rest stop parking lot.

The hunt for the snipers had ended, but the FBI's role in the case was far from over. The Bureau spent many more hours gathering evidence and preparing it for court—work that ultimately paid off in the convictions of both Muhammad and Malvo.

FBI evidence experts map the crime scene at one of the sniper shootings

FAMOUS CASES

Tennessee Waltz: The Dance is Over

*B*ribery. Bagmen. Crooked politicians. Ethical lapses.
All ugly terms that were part of a major FBI public corruption case lasting nearly six years.

In April 2008, the undercover sting known as "Tennessee Waltz" (coincidentally, also the official state song) ended where it started: a contractor working in the Shelby County Juvenile Court Clerk's Office was sentenced for his role in a corrupt invoice scam, accepting money for work never performed. He was the 12th and final subject brought to justice in the case.

Tennessee Waltz was a landmark investigation: it not only led to the convictions or guilty pleas of a dozen state and local public officials—including several state senators, a state representative, two county commissioners, and two school board members—but also to new state ethics laws and the creation of an independent ethics commission in Tennessee.

It began in May 2002, when the FBI's office in Memphis opened an investigation into reports of fraud and corruption in the Juvenile Court Clerk's Office. One of the individuals that agents questioned—a well-known lobbyist who was consulting for that office—admitted to wrongdoing and agreed to cooperate, wearing a wire to record conversations with suspects.

It wasn't long before an employee in the clerk's office who claimed to be a close acquaintance of several state legislators approached this lobbyist. The employee advised the lobbyist that he was a "bagman" for these politicians—and that, in exchange for money, these lawmakers would vote on legislation that would benefit the lobbyist's clients.

So the corruption investigation expanded—from local government to the state legislature. In the fall of 2003, the FBI launched an undercover operation to address what appeared to be a widespread public corruption problem.

As part of the operation, agents set up a fictitious company that recycled surplus electronic equipment to third world countries. They let it be known that they wanted legislation that would benefit their company and that they wanted exclusive contracts with local governments. The undercover agents offered bribes to individuals who—based on FBI information—investigators believed would take the money. And these individuals did take it, and then they told their colleagues, who in some instances took bribes as well.

Some of the corrupt politicians even introduced legislation that the FBI had drafted (but no legislation was ever passed). All told, agents paid out more than $150,000 in bribe money by the time the undercover portion of Tennessee Waltz ended in 2005.

The case, worked with the help of the Tennessee Bureau of Investigation, is one of the FBI's most successful examples to date involving the use of lawful sensitive techniques like undercover operations to investigate allegations of systemic corruption.

Public corruption continues to be the FBI's top criminal priority—and for good reason. Graft and greed in government not only waste billions in tax dollars, but also undermine democracy and threaten national security. In April 2008, the Bureau had more than 2,500 pending cases—an increase of 50 percent from 2003. In the previous two years, the FBI's work with a range of partners led to the conviction of more than 1,800 government officials.

An FBI agent (seated) gives cash to a Tennessee official in June 2005 as part of the undercover sting

FAMOUS CASES

Terrorism Case Roundup

Preventing terrorist attacks and dismantling terrorist networks is the FBI's top post-9/11 priority—and the most important measure by which it is judged. For the Bureau, that mandate has taken many different shapes and resulted in a large number of successes over the past seven years. Working with partners both here and overseas, the FBI has headed off developing plots by homegrown cells in the U.S.; helped take out key terrorist operatives overseas through key bits of intelligence and information; cut off terrorist funding and rounded up financiers; and taken off the streets a number of extremists who planned to provide or had already provided logistical or other support to terrorist networks.

Just a few examples:

The Portland Seven

Eighteen days after the 9/11 attacks, a group of men were found taking target practice in southwestern Washington State by a sheriff acting on a tip. The ensuing investigation uncovered an international terrorist cell operating in the Portland, Oregon area that was planning to attack American troops in Afghanistan. Seven individuals—including six Americans—were arrested and indicted; six were convicted and a seventh killed in Pakistan.

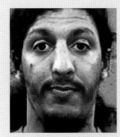

Richard Reid

The Shoe Bomber

On December 11, 2001, a British citizen named Richard Reid was subdued by passengers aboard a flight from Paris to Miami after he tried to ignite a bomb hidden in his black, high-top shoes. An extensive FBI investigation—which included recreating the powerful impact the bomb could have had on the airplane—ultimately led to his conviction and life sentence.

The Lackawanna Six

In June 2003, the last of six men from upstate New York—all Americans of Yemeni descent—pled guilty to providing material support to al Qaeda. At the urging of a known al Qaeda leader, they had traveled to bin Laden's al Farooq terrorist training camp in Afghanistan in the summer of 2001, where they had been trained in firearms and explosives. The investigation not only successfully dismantled an al Qaeda cell in the U.S., it also neutralized a major al Qaeda link to the Middle East and helped deter other potential attacks through information provided by the six individuals.

The Virginia Jihad

This investigation dismantled a radical cell operating in the Northern Virginia area under the inspiration of the Pakistan-based group Lashkar-e-Tayyiba. The group was well trained and violently anti-American, and some of its members had traveled to Pakistan and attended terrorist training camps, fully intending to join the Taliban and fight against U.S. forces in Afghanistan. The investigation resulted in the conviction of 11 people on terrorism charges, led to the apprehension and conviction of two terrorist subjects in London, contributed to the arrest of three individuals in Australia, and supported a terrorism case in France.

Khalid Shaikh Mohammed

Khalid Shaikh Mohammed

He was al Qaeda's operational mastermind, the primary architect of the 9/11 attacks, and the inspiration and driving force behind terrorist plots that killed thousands of people around the world. Based in part on information provided by the FBI and its partners, Mohammed was arrested in a predawn raid in Pakistan on March 1, 2003. He has since outlined his role in dozens of plots (including the murder of U.S. journalist Daniel Pearl) and provided a wealth of information that led the FBI and its counterparts to still more terrorists—including Hambali, the top al Qaeda strategist in Southeast Asia and the leader of the terrorist organization Jemmaah Islamiyah.

Jose Padilla

Jose Padilla

In May 2002, FBI agents arrested Jose Padilla, aka Abdullah al Muhajir, in Chicago. Padilla was later convicted—along with two other men—of being part of a North American terrorist support cell designed to send money, physical assets, and radical recruits to overseas conflicts. The cell operated out of many cities in the U.S. and Canada and coordinated with other terrorist groups waging violent jihad.

Trouble in Toledo

An Ohio truck driver from Kashmir named Iyman Faris first came to the FBI's attention through a foreign source that linked him to terrorists plotting attacks during Millennium celebrations. Through a subsequent investigation, including an interview with

Iyman Faris

Faris in March 2003, the Bureau learned that Faris was something of an operational scout for al Qaeda. He later admitted that he had met personally with bin Laden, discussed plots to attack the U.S. with Khalid Shaikh Mohammed, and cased the Brooklyn Bridge with an eye toward planning an attack. He was sentenced to 20 years in prison in October 2003. Faris also had connections to Nuradin Abdi, who was convicted of providing material support to terrorists, and Christopher Paul, who pled guilty in June 2008 to conspiring to use a weapon of mass destruction against targets in the U.S. and Europe.

The Torrance Plot
When police arrested two men in Torrance, California in what appeared to be a routine gas station robbery, they found evidence linking the pair to terrorism. The tip went to the FBI's Joint Terrorism Task Force in Los Angeles, which uncovered a violent plot by three U.S. citizens and a Pakistani national to attack military facilities, an Israeli consulate and airline, and Jewish synagogues in the area. By the time it was discovered, the scheme was fairly advanced: the plotters had scoped out targets, conducted surveillance, purchased weapons, and begun firearms training. The men were indicted in August 2005; the ringleader later pled guilty.

Domestic Successes
On the domestic front, the FBI has had its share of successes as well—heading off homegrown terrorist attacks by lone wolves like Gale Nettles—who plotted to blow up the 28-story federal courthouse in Chicago—and Demetrius Van Crocker—an anti-government fanatic who wanted to build and use a dirty bomb. And the Bureau has dealt substantial blows to eco- and animal-rights terrorists nationwide with a series of successful investigations, including "Operation Backfire," which consolidated cases from seven FBI field offices into a major initiative targeting acts of domestic terrorism in several states.

U.K. Airline Scheme
In August 2006, British authorities arrested more than 20 extremists who were believed to be actively planning to blow up airline flights to the U.S. over the Atlantic Ocean. The FBI worked closely with British and Pakistani law enforcement and intelligence agencies to identify key members of the cell and to stop them before they could strike, as well as to investigate their potential ties to America.

Spring '07 Plots Foiled
In early June 2007, four individuals—including a member of the parliament of Guyana—were arrested in three different countries for conspiring to blow up fuel tanks and pipelines at J.F.K. International Airport in New York. Just a few weeks earlier, an undercover FBI investigation had led to the arrest of six men who were allegedly amassing a small arsenal to attack the Fort Dix U.S. Army base in New Jersey and to "kill as many soldiers as possible." One of the men later pled guilty to weapons charges.

Holiday Nightmare
In November 2007, a 22-year-old Muslim convert named Derrick Shareef pled guilty to plotting to set off grenades at an Illinois shopping mall during the previous holiday season. The FBI arrested him following an undercover sting.

Above: Items seized from the home of Demetrius Van Crocker included components to build chemical and pipe bombs.
Left: Demetrius Van Crocker was arrested in 2004 after he attempted to obtain sarin nerve gas and C-4 explosives from an undercover FBI agent (samples shown here).

Selected Bibliography

Beyond materials in FBI files, the following works were found most useful in writing this book:

Batvinis, Raymond J. *The Origins of FBI Counterintelligence.* Lawrence, Kansas: University of Kansas Press, 2007.

Bonavolonta, Jules, and Brian Duffy. *The Good Guys: How We Turned the FBI 'Round – and Finally Broke the Mob.* New York: Simon & Schuster, 1996.

Burrough, Bryan. *Public Enemies: America's Greatest Crime Wave and the Birth of the FBI, 1933-34.* New York: Penguin Press, 2004.

Cummings, Homer, and Carl McFarland. *Federal Justice: Chapters in the History of Justice and the Federal Executive.* New York: The Macmillan Company, 1937.

DeLoach, Cartha D. "Deke." *Hoover's FBI: The Inside Story by Hoover's Trusted Lieutenant.* Washington, DC: Regnery Publishing, Inc., 1995.

Garrow, David J. *The FBI and Martin Luther King, Jr.: From "Solo" to Memphis.* New York: W.W. Norton & Company, 1981.

Jensen, Joan M. *The Price of Vigilance.* Chicago: Rand McNally & Company, 1968.

Kelley, Clarence M., and James Kirkpatrick Davis. *Kelley: The Story of an FBI Director.* Kansas City, Missouri: Andrews, McMeel & Parker, 1987.

Kessler, Ronald. *The Terrorist Watch: Inside the Desperate Race to Stop the Next Attack.* New York: Crown Forum, 2007.

Lamphere, Robert J., and Tom Schactman. *The FBI-KGB War: A Special Agent's Story.* New York: Random House, 1986.

Pistone, Joseph D., and Richard Woodley. *Donnie Brasco: My Undercover Life in the Mafia.* New York: New American Library, 1987.

Powers, Richard Gid. *Secrecy and Power: The Life of J. Edgar Hoover.* New York: The Free Press, 1987.

Hearings before the Senate Select Committee to Study Governmental Operations with Respect to Intelligence Activities. Volume 6, Federal Bureau of Investigation and *Book III: Supplementary Detailed Staff Reports on Intelligence Activities and the Rights of Americans.* Washington, D.C.: U.S. Government Printing Office, 1976.

Simeone, John, and David Jacobs. *The Complete Idiot's Guide to the FBI.* Indianapolis, Indiana: Alpha Books, 2003.

Theoharis, Athan G., et al. *The FBI: A Comprehensive Reference Guide.* Phoenix, Arizona: Oryx Press, 1999.

Turchie, Terry D., and Kathleen M. Puckett. *Hunting the American Terrorist: The FBI's War on Homegrown Terror.* Palisades, New York: History Publishing Company, 2007.

Benson, Robert Louis, and Michael Warner. *Venona: Soviet Espionage and the American Response, 1939-1957.* Washington, D.C.: National Security Agency and Central Intelligence Agency, 1996.

Whitehead, Don. *The FBI Story: A Report to the People.* New York: Random House, 1956.

FBI Directors, *1908-2008*

Stanley W. Finch,
1908-1911

When a "special agent force" was created in the summer of 1908, Stanley Finch—the Chief Examiner at the Department of Justice—was placed in charge. Finch oversaw the early Bureau and its growth under the White Slave Traffic Act of 1910. He placed so much importance in the enforcement of this law that he left the Bureau in 1911 and became Special Commissioner for the Suppression of White Slave Traffic.

Alexander Bruce Bielaski,
1911-1919

In 1911, A. Bruce Bielaski became head of the Bureau, managing Neutrality Act violations and other national security matters as they became Bureau priorities. He led the organization through World War I and oversaw its rise to become America's domestic counterintelligence agency.

William J. Flynn,
1919-1921

Former New York Secret Service Agent William Flynn was appointed Chief of the Bureau in 1919 and was charged with stopping the terrorist attacks that plagued the nation following the end of World War I.

William J. Burns,
1921-1924

Head of an international detective agency and a famed former Secret Service Agent, William Burns was appointed Director with the mission to reform the Bureau's operations and reduce its workforce in an era of tightening budgets. He created the first training program for new agents and oversaw a number of other reforms, many led by his assistant, J. Edgar Hoover. At the request of Attorney General Harlan Fiske Stone, Burns resigned in 1924 because of his role in the Teapot Dome Scandal.

J. Edgar Hoover,
1924-1972

Appointed in the wake of a political scandal that brought down his predecessor, J. Edgar Hoover deserves the lion's share of the credit for making the Bureau what it is today. He served as Director for 48 years—the longest of any FBI Director or other government leader. Along the way, he molded the FBI's investigative and intelligence capabilities and helped preserve national security and stability during the lawless gangster years, World II and the Cold War, and the tumultuous 1960s. Although his reputation was tarnished by mistakes and controversies in his later years, his vision of law enforcement professionalism and scientific-crime fighting, tempered by the need to uphold the Constitution, remain staples of the FBI and of police work to this day.

Clarence M. Kelley,
1973-1978

Clarence Kelley was the first Director to rise through the ranks of FBI, joining as an agent and rising to the rank of Special Agent in Charge. He later left the Bureau to serve as the Chief of Police in Kansas City, Missouri, where he was a noted innovator. Taking the reigns of the FBI in the midst of the Watergate crisis, Kelley led the Bureau through some of its darkest years, insisting that the organization maintain Hoover's vision of professionalism while pursuing quality investigations that took advantage of the FBI's national scope and ability to run long-term, highly complex cases.

William H. Webster,
1978 to 1987

Building on Kelley's work, former U.S. Attorney and federal judge William Webster continued the fight against mobsters and crooked politicians as the Bureau applied lessons learned from the intense scrutiny and criticism of the post-Watergate era. Under Webster, the FBI's national security focus grew as well, with many successful spy investigations and a rising response to global terrorism and drug trafficking. In 1987, Webster left the FBI after being asked to reform the CIA following the Iran-Contra scandal.

William S. Sessions,
1987 to 1993

Like Judge Webster, William Sessions came to the Bureau from the federal bench. Following the collapse of the Iron Curtain in the early 1990s, Sessions led the FBI through a significant shift in priorities, adjusting national security strategies and placing more emphasis on burgeoning violent crime. He also led technical innovations in DNA analysis and strengthened the Bureau's focus on white-collar crime.

Louis J. Freeh,
1993 to 2001

A former special agent and federal judge, Louis Freeh began his tenure as Director with a clearly articulated agenda focused on deepening and evolving crime problems both at home and abroad. Recognizing the growing globalization of crime, he responded by greatly enhancing foreign partnerships and doubling the number of FBI offices overseas. Freeh also guided the Bureau through increasing investigations of domestic and international terrorism and created new programs and initiatives to address the rise of cyber crime.

Robert S. Mueller,
September 4, 2001 to Present

Former federal prosecutor Robert Mueller was sworn into office with a mandate to strengthen the overall management of the FBI. One week later, the events of 9/11 gave the Bureau a new overriding mission—to prevent terrorist attacks and dismantle terrorist networks worldwide. In response, Mueller led a far-reaching transformation, massively upgrading the Bureau's counterterrorism operations and turning the FBI into an intelligence-led national security agency. He also spearheaded major improvements in information technology, lifted Bureau partnerships to new levels, and elevated the importance of investigating and preventing cyber attacks.

FBI Heritage

The Origins of the Special Agent Title

The title of special agent has been used in the Department of Justice since 1872, when Congress appropriated funds for "the detection and prosecution of crimes." Using these funds, Attorney General George Williams appointed an agent in the Department to conduct "special" investigations on his behalf. Other government law enforcement agencies may have occasionally used a similar title, but apparently none used it for an extended period of time.

By 1879, the Department of Justice title was changed to general agent, a supervisory role (this position was abolished in 1907). In 1894, a new special agent position was created under the general agent, investigating violations of the Indian Intercourse Act regulating trade with reservations. Secret Service personnel who were borrowed on a case-by-case basis handled the bulk of Justice Department investigations between 1879 and 1908.

In 1907, the year before the Bureau of Investigation (the FBI's precursor) was created, there were three special agents in the Justice Department: one investigated antitrust matters, one handled investigations related to the government's defense of suits before the Spanish Treaty Claims Commission, and one continued to handle Indian Intercourse Act violations.

In 1908 when Attorney General Charles Bonaparte reorganized the Department's investigators into a "special agent force," he hired nine Treasury investigators as special agents and put them together with 13 peonage investigators and 12 bank examiners. Whether all or some of the peonage investigators were called special agents is not known. The bank examiners were accountants and were originally called "special examiners." A distinction immediately arose between special agents and special examiners. This distinction existed into the 1930s, when it was decided that all investigative agents—agents and accountants—were to be called special agents.

Evolution of the FBI Badge

The first badge of the Bureau of Investigation was issued in 1909, shortly after the organization was given its first name. By 1913, there were 219 agents carrying this badge.

Shortly after J. Edgar Hoover was named Director of the Bureau in 1924, discussions began on adopting a new special agent badge. Many designs were considered. The pattern ultimately selected featured a miniature shield crested by an eagle. This badge was issued in May 1927. These first shield badges were slightly smaller than the present-day badge and had a flat facial surface.

The Bureau's name was changed to the Division of Investigation by the end of 1933, and momentum for a new badge design grew. At a national conference in Washington, D.C., special agents voted unanimously to retain the same style of badge but to have its size increased and to cast it with a slight curvature. The badges modeled in this fashion were first created in April 1934, but were in use for less than two years before changing a final time.

The design of today's FBI badge was adopted in 1935, when the organization was renamed the Federal Bureau of Investigation. The new badges were first manufactured by the Robbins Company of Attleboro, Massachusetts and were numbered from one to 1,000. Some of these original numbered badges may still be in use today, as they have been returned by retiring agents and reissued to incoming agents.

1908

1927

1934

1935

Present

The FBI Seal

Over the years, the FBI seal has undergone several significant changes. In its early years, the Bureau used the Department of Justice seal. The first official FBI seal was adopted in 1935, modifying the Department of Justice logo by adding "Federal Bureau of Investigation" and "Fidelity, Bravery, and Integrity" to the outer band. In 1940, Special Agent Leo Gauthier—a draftsman, artist, and illustrator—presented a new design based on an earlier Bureau flag that he had created. This design was readily accepted and has been the Bureau's symbol ever since.

Each element of the seal has a particular significance: The dominant blue field of the seal and the scales on the shield represent justice. The endless circle of 13 stars denotes unity of purpose as exemplified by the original 13 states. The laurel leaf has, since early civilization, symbolized academic honors, distinction, and fame. There are 46 leaves in the two branches, since there were 46 states in the Union when the FBI was founded in 1908. The significance of the red and white parallel stripes lies in their colors. Red traditionally stands for courage, valor, and strength, while white conveys cleanliness, light, truth, and peace. As in the American flag, the red bars exceed the white by one. The motto "Fidelity, Bravery, Integrity" succinctly describes the motivating force behind the men and women of the FBI. The peaked beveled edge that circumscribes the seal symbolizes the severe challenges confronting the FBI and the ruggedness of the organization. The gold color in the seal conveys the richness of the FBI's history and mission.

Fidelity, Bravery, Integrity–The FBI Motto

The origins of the FBI's motto are traced to a brief comment by Inspector W. H. Drane Lester, the editor of the Bureau employee magazine, *The Investigator*, in September 1935:

"F B I"

At last we have a name that lends itself to dignified abbreviation—the Federal Bureau of Investigation, which quite naturally becomes "F B I."

In the past our nicknames, which the public are so prone to give us, have been many and varied. "Justice Agents," "D. J. Men," "Government Men" are but a few of them, with the Bureau itself incorrectly referred to as "Crime Bureau," "Identification Bureau," and "Crime Prevention Bureau." The latest appellation, and perhaps the one which has become most widespread, is "G-Men," an abbreviation itself for "Government Men."

But "F B I" is the best and one from which we might well choose our motto, for those initials also represent the three things for which the Bureau and its representatives always stand: "Fidelity – Bravery – Integrity."

Drane Lester

Hall of Honor

FBI Agents Killed as the Direct Result of an Adversarial Action

The FBI honors its special agents killed in the line of duty as the result of a direct adversarial force or at the hand of an adversary. The names of these agents, who are appropriately termed "Service Martyrs," are included on a permanent plaque so that their ultimate sacrifice will always be remembered. The inscription on this Service Martyr Plaque reads: "In memory of Special Agents of the Federal Bureau of Investigation who were killed in the line of duty as the direct result of an adversarial action." A total of 35 agents had been so designated as of May 2008.

Edwin C. Shanahan
1898 - 1925

Paul E. Reynolds
1899 - 1929

Raymond J. Caffrey
1902 - 1933

W. Carter Baum
1904 - 1934

Samuel P. Cowley
1899 - 1934

Herman E. Hollis
1903 - 1934

Nelson B. Klein
1898 - 1935

Wimberly W. Baker
1910 - 1937

Truett E. Rowe
1904 - 1937

William R. Ramsey
1903 - 1938

Hubert J. Treacy, Jr.
1913 - 1942

Joseph J. Brock
1908 - 1952

John Brady Murphy
1917 - 1953

Richard Purcell Horan
1922 - 1957

Terry R. Anderson
1924 - 1966

Douglas M. Price
1941 - 1968

Anthony Palmisano
1942 - 1969

Edwin R. Woodriffe
1941 - 1969

Gregory W. Spinelli
1949 - 1973

Jack R. Coler
1947 - 1975

Ronald A. Williams
1947 - 1975

Johnnie L. Oliver
1944 - 1979

Charles W. Elmore
1945 - 1979

Jared Robert Porter
1935 - 1979

Robin L. Ahrens
1952 - 1985

Jerry L. Dove
1956 - 1986

Benjamin P. Grogan
1933 - 1986

L. Douglas Abram
1942 - 1990

John L. Bailey
1942 - 1990

Martha Dixon Martinez
1959 - 1994

Michael John Miller
1953 - 1994

William Christian, Jr.
1946 - 1995

Charles Leo Reed
1951 - 1996

Leonard W. Hatton
1956 - 2001

Barry L. Bush
1954 - 2007

FBI Agents Who Gave Their Lives
in the Performance of a Law Enforcement Duty

The FBI also honors those agents who lose their lives in the performance of their duty, but not necessarily during an adversarial confrontation. This would include situations involving "hot pursuit" of criminals and when death results from the agent taking immediate action to save one or more lives. A separate plaque memorializing the sacrifice of these agents reads: "In memory of Special Agents of the Federal Bureau of Investigation who lost their lives in the performance of a law enforcement duty." A total of 16 agents had been added to this list as of April 2008.

Albert L. Ingle
1903 - 1931

Percy E. Foxworth
1906 - 1943

Harold Dennis Haberfeld
1912 - 1943

Richard Blackstone Brown
1916 - 1943

Trenwith S. Basford
1916 - 1977

Mark A. Kirkland
1944 - 1977

Robert W. Conners
1946 - 1982

Charles L. Ellington
1946 - 1982

Terry Burnett Hereford
1948 - 1982

Michael James Lynch
1947 - 1982

James K. McAllister
1951 - 1986

Scott K. Carey
1952 - 1988

Stanley Ronquest, Jr.
1939 - 1992

Paul A. LeVeille
1959 - 1999

Robert R. Hardesty
1965 - 2005

Gregory J. Rahoi
1968 - 2006